THE
REAL WORLD
OF
DEMOCRACY
REVISITED

THE
REAL WORLD
OF
DEMOCRACY
REVISITED

And Other Essays on Democracy and Socialism

FRANK CUNNINGHAM

HUMANITIES PRESS
NEW JERSEY

First published in 1994 by
Humanities Press International, Inc.
165 First Avenue, Atlantic Highlands, New Jersey 07716

© Frank Cunningham, 1994

Library of Congress Cataloging-in-Publication Data
Cunningham, Frank, 1940–
The real world of democracy revisited, and other essays on
democracy and socialism / Frank Cunningham.
    p.   cm.
Includes bibliographical references and index.
ISBN 0-391-03837-0 (cloth). — ISBN 0-391-03838-9 (pbk.)
1. Democracy. 2. Communist state. 3. Socialism. I. Title.
JC423.C79 1994
321.8—dc20   93-14234
CIP

A catalog record for this book is available from the British Library.

Printed in the United States of America

Contents

Acknowledgments

Portions of this text have been previously published in the following publications, all of whom have graciously granted permission to reprint.

Interview: "C. B. Macpherson on Marx," *Socialist Studies: 1983* (Winnipeg: University of Manitoba Publications, 1984), 7–12.

"Democracy and Marxist Political Culture," Socialist Studies Annual No. 7, Jos Roberts and Jesse Vorst, eds., *Socialism in Crisis?: Canadian Perspectives* (Winnipeg: Fernwood Publishing, 1992), 107–15. Copies of this publication are available from The Society for Socialist Studies, 471 University College, University of Manitoba, Winnipeg, MB, 3RT 2M8.

"Democratic-Socialist Continua: Good and Bad," *Critica Marxista*, Vol. 27, No. 6 (November/December 1989), 19–35. The Italian title of the article partially reproduced here is "Democrazia e socialismo: problemi di metodo."

"Democracy and Socialism: Philosophical *Aporiae*," *Philosophy & Social Criticism*, Vol. 16, No. 4 (1990), 269–89.

"Community, Democracy, and Socialism," *Praxis International*, Vol. 11, No. 3 (October 1991), 310–16, Blackwell Publications.

"Radical Philosophy and the New Social Movements," in Roger Gottlieb, ed., *Tradition, Counter-Tradition, Politics* (Philadelphia: Temple University Press, 1993), 199–220.

"Democracy, Socialism, and the Globe." Reprinted from: *On the Track of Reason: Essays in Honor of Kai Nielsen*, Rodger Beehler, David Copp, and Béla Szabados, eds., 1992, by permission of Westview Press, Boulder, Colorado.

Preface

The title of this collection refers to C. B. Macpherson's published lectures, *The Real World of Democracy*,[1] in which he took stock of prospects for democracy in each of the capitalist, socialist, and developing worlds. As in his other works, Macpherson articulated a vision of democratic progress incorporating socialist equality and superseding procapitalist political culture and economic structures. Much has changed since 1965 when these lectures were given, but as the lead essay of this collection argues, Macpherson's project is far from outmoded. On the contrary, changes in the formerly socialist world and a rapidly if problematically shrinking globe make his approach to democratic political theory all the more urgent.

Like my earlier *Democratic Theory and Socialism*,[2] much of the specific content of these essays also owes a debt to Macpherson, whose orientation seems to me the best place to start in approaching a range of democratically problematic issues. However, it would be both misleading and presumptuous of me to try to construct what Macpherson himself might have thought about a world so dramatically changed after his death in 1987. Rather, drawing on work by him and by other democratic and socialist theorists, I identify a selection of problems relating to democracy and socialism and thrown into relief by the fall of the authoritarian, Communist regimes.

In these exercises I employ what I called in my earlier work "philosophy of the middle range." Agnosticism is maintained about whether foundational philosophical questions can be answered. Nor is the current debate joined over whether even trying to answer questions of philosophical basics leads to political dogmatism or is an otherwise flawed enterprise. Instead, the theoretical dimensions of some rather large political problems are identified, with respect to which crucial terms such as "socialism," "democracy,"

ix

and "equality" are prescriptively defined and some hypotheses are advanced about how to approach them. The problems are thereby addressed in a "pieces of puzzles" manner without pretense that deep philosophical grounding has provided final resolutions.

With the exception of the first essay, all the contributions to this work have been previously published in some form. But unlike many such collections, each has also been rewritten, in some cases extensively, to make for continuity and to reflect my current thinking. Though the essays contain references to one another and to the earlier book, each is sufficiently self-contained to be read in isolation. Thus a certain amount of repetition has been retained, but not, I think, a tedious amount. Essays 2 and 3 are of a more summary nature than the others and may therefore be good starting places for readers not immersed in democratic-socialist literature. Beyond this there is a logic to the organization of the essays, but as I have forgotten exactly what it is, other readers are invited to begin with whatever specific topics are of interest to them.

Acknowledgments of helpful comments are made in each essay, since I profited from the reactions of different friends and colleagues to the essays' various topics. The book's themes have also formed the core of courses in the Faculty of Philosophy at the University of Amsterdam in 1990 and in the Department of Political Science at the University of Toronto in 1991 and 1992. I owe a large debt of gratitude to the enthusiastic participation of students in these courses, their critical acumen and insights. Thanks are also due to Stephen Bronner for encouraging publication of the collection and to Keith Ashfield and the staff of Humanities Press for their contribution to the finished product.

TORONTO
MARCH 1993

Notes

1. Crawford Brough Macpherson, *The Real World of Democracy* (Toronto: Canadian Broadcasting Corporation, 1965). I have used the most recent of many reprintings (Concordia, Ont.: Anasi Press, 1992).
2. Frank Cunningham, *Democratic Theory and Socialism* (Cambridge: Cambridge University Press, 1987).

ESSAY 1

The Real World of Democracy Revisited

Already perplexing enough to any political theorist honest enough to admit it, the world became yet more puzzling for socialists after the collapse of late socialism in and around 1989. This is obviously so for those who supported the deposed regimes. It poses somewhat different challenges to socialists who were critical of the authoritarian governments, as freed peoples turned to forms of capitalism that might have been fashioned by Adam Smith, and the imposed internal peace of earlier years gives way to ethnic and national conflict.

Even nonsocialists must find the world recalcitrant to understanding based on their theories: The collapse of socialism was not supposed to result in economic crises and general political malaise in developed capitalism. Further, while overcoming poverty in an environmentally sustainable way in the postcolonial countries is generally recognized as urgent for everyone, its attainment remains elusive. This creates another challenge for all political theorists who want their views to bear on global realities.

In his 1965 published radio lectures, "The Real World of Democracy,"[1] C. B. Macpherson approached global situations, partly similar to those of today and partly different, from the standpoint of his unique version of democratic-socialist theory. Macpherson speculated on the prospects for

Versions of this paper were read between February and November of 1992 at the Karl Polanyi Institute of Concordia University, the Departments of Sociology and Philosophy at Rice University, and the Department of Philosophy at Columbia University. I am grateful to Alkis Kontos and to participants in these sessions for helpful comments and criticisms.

1

democratic progress, not just regarding "first world" liberal democracies, but also regarding the socialist "second" and the newly developing "third" worlds as well. Noteworthy about the lectures are Macpherson's hopeful projections. At the risk of giving aid and comfort to foes of his effort to wed democracy and anticapitalism, this essay will take stock of his prognoses— they have not fared very well—to exhibit what I see as the enduring strength of his orientation to the political world and to suggest some places where emendation is in order.

One reason to take Macpherson's views as a point of departure is precisely that he dared thus to speculate, and enough time has gone by that lessons might be learned by estimating the impact of world developments for the theoretical views behind his speculation. Another reason is that Macpherson's theoretical views have already been found enormously helpful by many democratic theorists. Two of his central concepts—"possessive individualism" and the socialist "retrieval" of certain liberal-democratic ideals—have become influential components of contemporary democratic and socialist thinking. In *The Political Theory of Possessive Individualism*,[2] Macpherson argued that political philosophy from Hobbes through Locke should be seen as the promulgation of a concept of human nature whereby a person's worth is regarded as the ability to extract as much as possible from nature and other people to satisfy infinite desires for personal consumption. This picture of humanity conflicts with one where to be human is to develop uniquely human capacities in cooperation with others.

Democratic Theory: Essays in Retrieval,[3] published eleven years later in 1973, was the first of several collections of essays addressing the prospects for democratic progress in liberal democracy. On Macpherson's view this requires escaping a predominant market society ethos of competitive utility maximization to achieve a culture valuing the equal development of truly human capacities. Macpherson also called these human "powers," using this term to mean something like the essential potentialities Aristotle wrote of rather than brute abilities as focused on by his contemporary power-political "realists," whom he strongly criticized. Since liberal-democratic culture is not entirely dominated by an extractive concept of human nature but includes, in tension with the latter, a developmental conception as well, Macpherson saw grounds for optimism.

THE GLOBAL PROJECTIONS

It was from the perspective shaped by these and related concepts that Macpherson approached "The Real World of Democracy." As in his more detailed treatments of liberal democracy, Macpherson took a dynamic view. Rather than classifying social or political systems as simply democratic or nondemocratic, he identified pro- and antidemocratic aspects and prospects to produce democratic balance sheets for each of the three worlds. Macpherson saw the major democratic advantages of liberal-democratic capitalist countries to be the potential for control over government afforded by electoral politics and protection of individual rights. On the negative side are a competitive culture that inhibits cooperation and economic inequalities that stifle democratic participation. Each of these is sustained by predominantly market economies.

The major democratic impediments in the socialist world were the absence even of formal means for popular control of government and relative scarcity; while its main potential resided in material equality. Countries of the recently decolonized world enjoy what is lacking in either of the other two, the presence of a general will based in the shared project of nation building; the main inhibition Macpherson saw to democratization in this world is extreme scarcity. Potential for democracy in the developed capitalist world resides in making representative government more responsive. Democratic progress is possible in the second and third worlds, Macpherson thought, compatibly with single-party political systems, provided the parties became internally democratic and open. In all three worlds, representative democracy and party politics need to be supplemented with participatory democracy.

Macpherson foresaw democratic progress in each domain. This would be facilitated in the socialist and developing worlds by overcoming scarcity. Transition to a nonmarket and more participatory society would be sparked in the first world by the example of the "moral advantage" of socialist equality.[4] Evidently, these projections do not match current reality. Possessive individualism, inequality, and a market economy not only remain dominant features of the capitalist world, but it, and not socialist equality, has provided the model for peoples of both second and third world countries, who, given an opportunity, have voted against socialism and for an extreme version of market capitalism. Though Macpherson was aware of the antidemocratic features of paternalistic one-party rule, his death in 1987 spared him from what would have been disappointing revelations for him about gross and widespread abuse of power by leaders in socialist countries for personal gain. As well, he did not anticipate tribal and factional antagonisms in the third world or the resurgence of violent nationalism in Eastern Europe and the former Soviet Union.

Does this mean that Macpherson's political theories are disconfirmed? I shall approach this question in the same charitable spirit exhibited by

Macpherson himself in an interview on the occasion of the 100th anniversary of Marx's death on how well Marx's ideas stood the test of time. (It happens that the interview was conducted by myself; it is appended to this essay.) As the interview shows, Macpherson's charity was primarily motivated by reluctance to lose what he saw of continuing value in Marx's thought. An analogous aim motivates the present exercise. In particular, it seems to me that of the many ways one might try to comprehend the relations between socialism and democracy in a post-1989 world, Macpherson's theoretical orientation still provides the best starting place. As in the case of many theories, predictive failures serve rather to indicate directions for correction and supplementation than to mandate rejection.

MACPHERSON'S THEORETICAL FRAMEWORK

Some of Macpherson's influential concepts have already been alluded to—possessive individualism, the socialist retrieval of liberal democracy, and developmental versus extractive powers—to which may be added other core notions, such as a distinction between exclusionary versus enabling conceptions of property[5] and an idea of liberty stronger than the negative, liberal conception famously defended by Isaiah Berlin (where this is nothing more than freedom from the deliberate interference by others from satisfaction of present preferences) but weaker than an alternative of idealist philosophers according to which one could be "forced to be free."[6] The usefulness of these core concepts depends upon whether one is trying to employ them to make sense of that portion of the political world Macpherson addressed and whether his concerns about what political theory should be useful for are also shared. The full force of Macpherson's work is therefore missed, and some criticisms misplaced, if his contribution in locating a terrain and defining goals is not taken into account.[7]

Though he did not ignore economic and political-institutional arrangements, Macpherson's primary focus of attention was on political culture. He thus joined a relatively small number of political theorists on the centre and the left of the political spectrum (one thinks also of Gramsci or Marcuse) who have attempted to identify and name core motivating popular values and views of human nature; to exhibit tensions, contradictions, and other complexities and interrelations among them; and, by tracing origins, drawing out consequences, and offering persuasive definitions, to influence popular self-definitions. The aim of this exercise was explicitly prodemocratic. It should go without saying that Macpherson wanted to get his analyses of the origins of contemporary political culture historically right and to describe relevant economic and institutional matters accurately, but his historical and social-scientific efforts were always guided by the explicit goal of finding ways that democracy might be enhanced.

Economic matters are not introduced in this methodology as strict determinants. Macpherson was less concerned to explain the economic origins of possessive individualism in a causal manner than to exhibit the fit between this cultural phenomenon and market capitalism. Reference to scarcity is introduced not to explain undemocratic features of second and third world political life, but to identify a limit to democratic progress. Macpherson's goal and his approach to explanation come together in his use of "models" of alternative conceptions of liberal democracy. The function of a model in his terminology is to recommend something while exhibiting limitations to and possibilities for its realization.[8]

In addition to these conceptual and methodological elements of Macpherson's explanations, two features require special mention: *contextualization* and *ontology*. One respect in which the approach is contextual has already been alluded to. How democracy is promoted depends upon specific circumstances of the society within which this is desired; hence, democratic progress may be achieved in different ways in the three worlds addressed in the Massey Lectures. In a study of these lectures, Ernesto Laclau identifies a related aspect of Macpherson's contextualism, namely, its assumption of contingency.[9] This is most clearly evident in the historical demonstration that liberalism antedated liberal democracy and indeed was antagonistic to democratic progress.[10] When, therefore, democracy came to be understood as liberal democracy in the industrialized capitalist world, this meant that there was no *essential* association of these things and that alternative ways of articulating democratic ideals and projects, such as those treated in *The Real World of Democracy*, are possible.

Laclau's own deployment of contingent analysis aims to reject any suggestion of essential natures or relations.[11] It is thus in tension with Macpherson's endorsement of what he called "ontology." This refers to his views about conflicting conceptions of human nature. The importance of keeping ontological debates in view, Macpherson argued, is not just that our culture contains contradictory conceptions of the human essence (as infinite appropriator and as exerter of truly human powers), which have implications for democratic practice, but also that there exists what he saw as a contest between technological thinking and thought that addresses ontological matters. Contrary to the charges of critics who attribute to Macpherson a productivist faith in technological progress,[12] he feared that technological change can fail to lay the basis for democratic progress and even undermine it should an increasingly technological culture lose sight of questions about specifically human capabilities.[13]

MACPHERSON'S PERSPECTIVE AND THE FUTURE

Faced with the apparent lack of fit between projections in *The Real World of Democracy* and current political realities, somebody sympathetic to the core ideas of Macpherson's theories might react in any of several alternative ways. Pointing to economic and political chaos in the newly capitalist countries of late socialism, it might be argued that his predictions have not yet been proven false and that time will yet tell. Or it could be argued, again with reference to the formerly socialist world, that Macpherson simply underestimated the degree of scarcity or the strength of undemocratic structures which blocked democratic progress within it. Supplementing either of these attempts to save the theory, it might be said that the Gorbachev phenomenon was an effort to democratize the Soviet Union within a single party/state system, as Macpherson claimed is possible, and that had it not been for popular mistrust of anything even formally resembling the former regime and naiveté about the benefits of a capitalist market, Gorbachev could have succeeded.

Such speculations are not inappropriate. In my view, however, they should be classified along with the observation that Macpherson's projections were made in public radio lectures and during the Cold War, when it was important to counteract demonizing portraits of socialist countries, just as the persistence of neocolonialism made it important to humanize the developing world. The force of these considerations is to counteract any attempt to write off Macpherson's political-theoretical views as falsified relics of a bygone era. But they do not exonerate somebody sharing Macpherson's aims and attracted to the general contours of his approach from reexamining this theory to see where it needs to be altered or supplemented in order to carry the project forward in new world contexts. What is more, the "wait and see" attitude described above could participate in a stagnating pendulum effect, where politically oppressive authoritarianism and economically brutal capitalism alternate. Instead, democratic theory needs to contribute to freeing people from seeing these as exclusive alternatives.

Rethinking elements of Macpherson's perspective is required to shape it to one that can accommodate two, mainly post-1989, phenomena in the previously socialist world: the overwhelming and evidently strongly felt rejection of anything with socialist connotations and the pervasive and sometimes violent resurgence of nationalistic attitudes. Some of the suggestions proffered in this and subsequent essays in this collection will bear on the first and third worlds as well.

SOCIALISM

If, as many contemporary democratic socialists have been at pains to argue, socialism is necessary, if all too obviously not sufficient, to make major democratic progress,[14] then it is incumbent on the democrat to try to retrieve a culture where socialism and democracy are not thought essentially anti-thetical. Macpherson's approach to the ideal of socialism is at once too weak and too strong for this purpose. In *The Real World of Democracy*, he specifies equality as that about socialism which gives it a moral edge over capitalism, but the meaning of this term is not explicated nor is it made clear whether equality is essential to socialism or a product of something more essential.[15] From his other, more theoretical works, readers have reasonably taken as definitive of "socialism" Macpherson's alternative to a possessive individualist society, that is, his model of a nonmarket society in which the equal full development of truly human potentials is approximated.

Thus interpreted, Macpherson's approach to socialism does not articulate a specifically socialist ideal, named as such. Many contemporary democratic theorists would see this as an advantage. Not only has the term "socialism" become tainted and debased by decades of authoritarian rule, but, as nearly all socialists today insist, the notion of socialism, like that of social democracy, reform, revolution, or democracy itself, needs to be flexibly and imaginatively rethought. While agreeing on these points, it still seems to me that there are good reasons to retain the term.

In popular political thought it is undeniable that "socialism" carries authoritarian connotations. But it also carries connotations of anticapitalism. This makes the stance of somebody who criticizes capitalism on democratic grounds problematic. To abandon socialist discourse leaves its authoritarian interpretation intact, and I, for one, am not as sanguine as some that ideals and even practices associated with the late socialism could not in some form return. It also makes it difficult for the democrat to appropriate any feature of preexisting socialist ideals that represents a democratically important alternative to capitalism. In subsequent essays I shall argue that what Macpherson saw as of moral value in socialism, equality, should play this role.

It might be thought sufficient just to identify socialism with anticapitalism. But not everything of and pertaining to capitalism need be shunned by socialists, as Macpherson himself famously argued with respect to elements of liberal democracy. Another example pertains to markets. Macpherson was strongly critical of what he called market society, that is, a society the culture of which encouraged people to regard their own and others' capacities as salable commodities, but it is not clear how he regarded market *economies*. The demonstrated failings of socialist command economies indicate that a stand must be taken on the latter point and that room for economic markets must be retained in alternatives to capitalism. This makes important current debates (not joined in this collection) over just how and where markets might fit into a socialist economy. It also makes Macpherson's critique of market society all the more crucial for combatting the reproduction in popular culture of the market dimensions of an economy.

While not everything about capitalism is to be rejected by socialists as bad, neither should everything that is wrong in a capitalist society be attributed to capitalism *per se* and its alternative accordingly built into the notion of socialism. As the appended interview makes plain, Macpherson did not espouse a class-reductionist viewpoint, which especially lends itself to such a picture.[16] However, in the absence of an explicit treatment of the meaning of "socialism," there is a risk that his idea of the development of truly human capacities may become partially definitive of the term.

Essay 8 will argue that in a global context socialism has the potential to facilitate a certain analogue of Macpherson's eloquently described goal. But there are problems with the notion as an interpretation of socialism. Several critics otherwise sympathetic to Macpherson's project have resisted constructing a democratic-socialist political theory around any concept of what is essentially human.[17] They fear that this detracts from a pluralist conception of democracy and that if such a concept supposes possible harmony of human interests, as Macpherson agreed it did,[18] room for institutional means to address conflict would not be maintained.

These criticisms identify problems that need to be addressed (which is why in *Democratic Theory and Socialism* I attempted to add pluralism to Macpherson's retrievals and defined a "democratic ideal" by reference both to negotiation and consensus),[19] but there is a more pressing danger. Arguably, the major root of formerly existing socialism's demise was vanguardist paternalism, the logic of which cannot but lead to an antidemocratic, downward spiral.[20] Offensive enough to the paternalized in itself, paternalism becomes especially oppressive when it turns to thoroughgoing authoritarianism, thus centrally contributing to strong popular rejections of socialism in Eastern Europe and the former Soviet Union. One might grant that the mere propagation of a theory about the human essence does not necessitate paternalistic socialist politics, but it is hard to see how it could not facilitate such practice, especially if reference to development of a supposed essence is built into the meaning of "socialism."

Macpherson's comments in the appended interview, among other places,[21] make it clear that he had no illusions about the counterproductive nature of vanguardism, but the fact remains that if there are truly human capacities then it may be possible not to act in accord with them, and policy aimed at avoiding this could only be carried out by those who know what the true human capacities are. The danger of playing into paternalism is more acute if one-party political systems are thought to be potentially democracy enhancing. Macpherson was aware of the danger, which is why he insisted on party democracy and openness. It seems to me, however, that Macpherson underestimated the extraordinary if not unbreachable obstacles to such a task.

Moreover, though in both the old and new capitalist worlds, most have now run for cover, there remain not a few socialist vanguardist theorists. In my experience the attraction of Macpherson to such theorists is his endorsement of single-party/state systems in the developing world. Perhaps this is partly due to a romanticized image of non-Western peoples, or one that chauvinistically views them as undifferentiated masses. In any case the generalized message is that political competition and protection of individual rights are luxuries inappropriate to hard times and strong political confrontation.

Some economic and political-scientific tasks are indicated for those in agreement with the observations above. It is easier to announce the compatibility of socialism and economic markets than to figure out how this could be arranged. Real existing multiparty politics have not always promoted democracy and have often inhibited it, so it is not enough simply to express scepticism about the democratic potentials of single-party systems. The essays of this collection aim to contribute to questions about the conceptualization of socialism, democracy, equality, and other such topics on the same, political-cultural terrain of interest to Macpherson, if not in the same style (and with no pretense of duplicating his breadth or erudition). Required in my view is more or less fine-grained attention to the notion of socialism and its relation to democracy. The aim is to retrieve a democratic-socialist ideal, while regarding socialism modestly as one moment in the project of expanding democracy.

NATIONALISM AND DEMOCRATIC PHILOSOPHY

Rather than dismissing "ontological" concerns about human nature, normatively considered, as some radical political theorists are wont to recommend, such concerns might be somewhat differently located than in Macpherson's theory. First, it will be appropriate to attend briefly to a large gap in the latter. Macpherson's forte was the analysis of specifically political-cultural phenomena, rather than of such other forces as religion and ethnic or national identification. Thus, regarding his own country, he addressed political populism in Alberta,[22] but not the national question of Quebec and its relation to English-speaking Canada. It should not be surprising, therefore, that little exists in Macpherson's conceptual resources to anticipate or to comprehend the resurgence of nationalism in the formerly socialist countries.

This resurgence poses a problem for democrats. One project of authoritarian socialism was to obliterate or at least to marginalize preexisting institutions and attitudes of civil society and to replace them with a new culture of what used to be called "socialist man." Democrats do not at all want to endorse such attacks. On the other hand, it is also difficult to sanction the often intolerant and sometimes violent nature that newly freed national sentiments have been taking. The dilemma can be traced in part to authoritarianism itself. The result of a socialist attack on traditions of civil society was only to drive them underground into mutually isolated and isolating privatized compartments, where their most intolerant dimensions were nurtured. But for a democrat who thinks it important to preserve pluralistic tolerance, the problem cannot be so easily confined. Any traditions and modes of life that define what counts as a good life for those who embrace them become democratically problematic when they conflict with one another or with democratic tolerance itself.

The problem is a mirror of the one raised by Macpherson's desire to identify truly human capacities as those that developmental democracy will promote. A democratic champion of tolerance must maintain formal democratic norms in the face of alternative and sometimes democracy-threatening substantive concepts of the good. A developmental democratic socialist must find a way to promote action in accord with a substantive concept of the good without inhibiting democratic pluralism. Macpherson, himself, only slightly addressed the question of pluralism, and contemporary communitarian/ individualist debates to which these sorts of conundrums are central did not shift into high gear until the very end of his life.[23]

As a matter of abstract methodology, the following seem to be polar strategies: A *philosophical* solution seeks to indicate directions for human development and prescribe limits to tolerance, justifying these by reference to supposed bases of morality, a description of the essence of humanity, or some other such foundational theory. Persuasion or force is then required to secure implementation. Alternatively, a *political* solution aims to free people as far as possible to develop their potentials as they see fit or to pursue traditional goods (or not pursue these), hoping that with provision of procedural, material, and cultural means to these activities there will be few occasions when adjudication will be necessary. When adjudication is nonetheless unavoidable, prescriptions are made on an *ad hoc* basis. The role, if required, of either persuasion or force is less prominent than on the philosophical approach, even though the capacities people choose to exercise or the goods they pursue may not conform to any philosopher's wishes.[24]

Following on the sad lesson of socialist paternalism, I favour a strategy at or near the second of these poles, but with some qualifications. First, one need not reject philosophy, even foundational philosophy, to adopt the political solution. Instead of debating the relative *importance* of philosophy and democratic politics, one might more fruitfully address their relative *locations*. It was urged above that "development of truly human capacities" should not be taken as partly definitive of "socialism." I should now like to urge as well that this not be taken as definitive of "democracy" either. In Essay 3 the question will be taken up about whether democracy (on any of several possible interpretations) should be regarded as an end in itself or as a means to other goals.

If the position is adopted that it is a means, then this leaves room for debate over what goals those who enjoy the possibilities afforded by life in a highly democratic society would be well advised to pursue. Philosophical considerations can play a role in such deliberations. They are called for as a result of successful democracy-promoting politics rather than as integral to determining what such politics is. (In Essays 5 and 7, to allude to points too involved to explicate here, it will be argued that, regarding specifically political philosophy, the converse relation does not obtain and that considerations of democratic theory and practice should play a role internal to the conduct of such philosophy.)

A second qualification is to insist that a democratic political orientation does not require one to give up making value judgments. A distinction needs to be drawn between appeal to commonly accepted values and justification of value judgments by philosophical theories of ethics. Procedures or *ad hoc* adjudications that reflect values become problematic from a democratic point of view only when there is no consensus on them. Some socialist theorists, like Kai Nielsen, maintain that since there is much more consensus about daily motivating moral values than about philosophical justifications, appeal to the former will suffice for nearly all practical purposes.[25]

"ONTOLOGY" AND POLITICAL "REALISM"

Nielsen's perspective is certainly in accord with Macpherson's insofar as each opposes a so-called realist approach to political theory and practice that shuns appeal to values. There may also be room for agreement regarding values and foundational justifications.[26] The truly human characteristics Macpherson actually lists are: "the capacity for rational understanding, for moral judgement and action, for aesthetic creation or contemplation, for the emotional activities of friendship and love, and, sometimes, for religious experience." He describes this as a nonexhaustive list, and adds that "whatever the uniquely human attributes are taken to be" they are regarded as "a satisfaction in themselves, not simply a means to consumer satisfactions."[27] The emphasis, therefore, is more on the self-motivating character of uniquely human attributes than on their specific content. Even regarding the specific list Macpherson produces, however, this seems just the sort of thing over which it should not be too difficult to find consensus (at least among the nonphilosophers, or indeed among the philosophers when they are not at their desks) without philosophical argumentation.[28]

MACPHERSON'S VIEWS AND OUR TIMES

Macpherson's emphasis on democracy as the guiding principle of socialist theory and his focus on specifically political-cultural dimensions of democracy put him in the forefront of radical thought in the 1960s, the 1970s, and well into the 1980s. I have argued in favour of retaining this framework as well as continuing to make use of key concepts and methods deployed by Macpherson: possessive individualism, socialist retrieval of liberal-democratic values, contextualization in the estimation of democratic possibilities, and other notions elaborated above. Undoubtedly challenged by dramatic world changes since the late 1980s, Macpherson's views, no less than those of other similarly influential political theorists, require critical adaptation to continue playing a fruitful role for those sharing his democratic aims.

In this essay I have indicated some directions I perceive for such adaptation (without suggesting that there may not be other appropriate responses). The collapse of the authoritarian regimes in Eastern Europe and the Soviet Union calls for closer treatment of the notion of socialism than Macpherson gave it. The resulting analysis should, it seems to me, modestly focus on the specifically egalitarian dimension of a socialist ideal rather than identifying it with the human "developmental" aim of democracy in general, and the analysis should profit from lessons of attempted vanguardism. The resilience of nationalist and other such identifications raises theoretical as well as practical questions and calls for reorientation of thinking about the relation between political and philosophical (Macpherson's "ontological") concerns in democratic-socialist theory. Subsequent essays in this collection will address aspects of these topics.

First it should be noted that despite lacunae and unforeseen world changes in Macpherson's 1965 reflections, he was in one respect decades ahead of his times. As indicated above, Macpherson criticized those who see the meaning of life in ever-increasing production of consumer goods. This "technological" orientation reinforces a morally objectionable self-image of humans as infinite, passive appropriators, thus cheapening the quality of life and defining human relations as essentially competitive. Macpherson's point is not just that this is wrong in itself, but that it also strains the legitimacy of liberal-democratic societies, both in the eyes of their citizens and of the world.[29]

In the sixth and last of the Massey Lectures, "The Near Future of Democracy and Human Rights," a similar point is made about international relations. Macpherson's concluding comment in *The Real World of Democracy* is the following exhortation:

> If you want an operative conclusion, it is this: tell your politicians that the free way of life depends, to an extent they have not yet dreamed of, on the Western nations remedying the inequality of human rights as between ourselves and the poor nations. Nothing less than massive aid, which will enable the poor nations to lift themselves to recognizable human equality, will conserve the moral stature and the power of the liberal democracies.[30]

Given the current crisis of global sustainability where a downward spiral of ecological degradation and gross imbalance of wealth is finally recognized as of emergency proportions, it is too bad that the liberal democracies did not heed Macpherson's advice.

APPENDIX

C. B. Macpherson
on Marx

On the 100th anniversary of Marx's death, Canada's Society for Socialist Studies had me interview Macpherson and the Canadian historian Stanley B. Ryerson on their views about Marxism. The interviews were published in *Socialist Studies: 1983* (Winnipeg: University of Manitoba Publications, 1984), 7–12. Below is the interview with Macpherson.

F.C.   *We have had a full century to examine Karl Marx's views, both as a theory and as embodied in social practice. How in your opinion has he stood the test of time?*

C.B.M.   I think remarkably well. If we take his analysis and prescriptions together, their apparent shortcomings or failures are more a matter of error in timetable than error of analysis. I refer to the error in expecting a breakdown of capitalism and its supersession by a new kind of society much earlier than in fact has happened. He did have at least spurts of hope, especially at the time of the Paris Commune, that the new society was just around the corner. But even in that matter of timetable we shouldn't lose sight of the fact that he was more concerned to argue about the long run, that is, to argue from his general theory of historical change and particularly the laws of motion of capitalism.

I think all that analysis has stood up well. Labour has become more alienating—the degradation of work, as Braverman calls it. There has been, of course, the increasing concentrations of capital that Marx foresaw. There have been increasingly severe recurrent economic crises, and so on. We have to allow for some factors that he couldn't really have foreseen 100 years ago: the uneven development of capitalism that brought revolution first not in the highly developed capitalist countries but in the ones that had suddenly been

14

pulled into the capitalist orbit and things of that sort. It's true that capitalism has been a lot more resilient than at least subsequent Marxists expected. But still, capitalism has been badly shaken, and where it still exists it has had to go on the defensive. It has been saved repeatedly, chiefly by war and cold war. But war presumably cannot go on saving capitalism indefinitely.

I should say the only serious doubt is about the adequacy of Marx's class analysis and about the adequacy of his consequent prescription of a proletarian revolution as the only possible mechanism of a transition to a good society. Clearly the proletariat in the most advanced capitalist countries has not become revolutionary. It hasn't turned out to be what he called the universal class—a class whose consciousness of its own alienation would turn into a revolutionary consciousness and into revolutionary action. The working class in North America and Britain at least is very far from that. It is still mainly devoted to fighting to maintain or increase its share of the capitalist pie, without, as I put it in something I wrote recently, questioning the methods of the bakery.

F.C.   *Some Marxists of a traditional sort have drawn the conclusion from what you have just said that we need to be patient, to wait until the sleeping giant wakes up, whereas some non-Marxists claim that once you admit this fact about lack of class consciousness you've proven that Marxism is simply wrong. How do you react to these views?*

C.B.M.   Well certainly I don't think we should just wait, and it seems to me there are already indications that a lot of people are not. A lot of people other than the classical proletarians are not prepared just to wait.

On the point about the proletariat not having turned out the way Marx seemed to have expected, I don't know that we ought to fault Marx too heavily. He is on record as having foreseen a change in the makeup of the proletariat, it seems to me, of the need for an old fashioned revolution. I am referring to his expectation, which unfortunately is just hinted at in the *Grundrisse*, that the great technological advances that will be made just because of the capitalist drive for profits will increasingly replace living labour with what he called congealed labour, namely capital now in a highly developed technological form. Production would be taken over, more and more, by new instruments and new sources of energy—automation and all that. Then, the source of profit would not be as now—the extraction of surplus value from living labour—but the increase of value produced by putting science and technology to work.

The point here is that this would produce a less oppressed and more educated and versatile working class. If the working class is likely to change in that direction, then one would no longer be counting on the utter grinding down of the proletariat, which is what we have usually thought Marx was relying on in all that talk about the universal class turning to revolution just because it was so totally exploited, totally alienated. Marx never pursued this other insight; so we don't know whether it would have led him to modify his view of the need for a proletarian revolutionary seizure of power, but in any case, a classical Marxian revolution now seems very unlikely in the advanced capitalist countries. I think Marxists ought to be exploring the possibilities of transition to the ultimate good society that Marx was after by other means and by means which I would hope would let us keep what is valuable in the liberal tradition, in liberal democracy.

F.C.   *This of course calls to mind your own work which has been closely associated with questions of liberal democracy. Could you tell us how you see Marx in relation to these questions? What of Marxism do you think would remain in a socialist perspective and practice embodying liberal democratic values?*

C.B.M.   Let me say first what I think is valuable in the liberal tradition. At the level of abstract theory it is something like John Stuart Mill's view of human nature as developmental, amounting to the full and free enjoyment and development of human capacities, everyone's capacities. This was seen to require quite a change away from existing social relations. This view of the essential nature of man seems to me virtually identical with Marx's ultimate humanistic vision. Marx was indeed sceptical of talk about the human essence, which usually implied an unchanging human nature. For Marx, of course, man makes himself, changes his own nature by changing his social relations. Hence Marx's remark that the human essence is in reality the ensemble of social relations. But this is in no way inconsistent with the developmental liberal vision. A socialist theory and practice which was faithful to Marx's humanistic vision would already embody that valuable element of liberal-democratic theory.

At the operative level, the liberal values that I want to see maintained are civil and political liberties: freedom of speech, association, publication, etc; freedom from arbitrary arrest and imprisonment; freedom to exert political pressures whether by the vote or in other ways, and in general, civil and political liberties at least of the degree that we have them now in the liberal-democratic states. I would like to see that core of the liberal tradition kept, and the question then is: can it be kept, can it be fused in any way with the Marxian analysis?

F.C.   *You know better than I that many Marxists think that the unique contribution of Marx to political theory was precisely to reject what you are outlining, that he was a collectivist as opposed to an individualist and that he rejected civil liberties as merely formal mechanisms which are taken advantage of by capitalists to serve their ends and to be thrown out when they stand in their way. Do you think that this is a false interpretation of Marx?*

C.B.M.   Yes, I do. False and unhistorical. Let me take it both on the abstract level and the operative level. On the abstract level I would say that Marx is an individualist in the basic sense that his ultimate vision was of a society where every individual could be a fully human being. On the operative level it's true that Marx was apt to scoff at the civil liberties of the bourgeois state and all the rest of the state apparatus, and perhaps that's due to the fact that he was living and writing at a time when liberal democracy really didn't exist yet. There was a liberal state in some countries, but it wasn't democratic. The liberalism of 19th century capitalism didn't really extend very much to the working class. Few of them had the vote, and as for freedom of assembly, they were certainly chopped down pretty fast when their freedom of assembly looked dangerous to those in power.

    No doubt that is the reason why Marx was able to dismiss civil liberties as a capitalist convenience. But with the subsequent growth of working class political muscle, the fact that they now all have the vote and have considerable power by their industrial organizations makes it harder to see the whole civil liberties package as just a convenience to capitalism. It may be that it is, but I would argue that it is also a necessity for any kind of democratic society in which the working class is going to have any place at all. If they couldn't organize, speak, publish, and so on, if they were denied the civil liberties they now have, never mind getting any more, it would simply set back the prospect of change toward socialism.

F.C.   *This raises the question about how a transition to a democratic socialist society is possible. Could you say something about this subject?*

C.B.M. Let me start by saying that I think Marx's prescription of revolutionary proletarian action and the dictatorship of the proletariat, the vanguard state, were things Marx had to prescribe by default, so to speak. That is, as I said a moment ago, when Marx wrote there were as yet in the world no liberal democracies really. There were a few liberal states, but they weren't anything like fully democratic, and so Marx's prescriptions of a revolutionary overthrow of the whole liberal state made sense. Of course even then there were his well-known possible exceptions for England, America and Holland. I don't put any particular weight on that because the reasons he gave, as Lenin pointed out later, ceased to operate within a few decades. I am simply saying that Marx's prescription of revolutionary proletarian dictatorship was never more than instrumental towards an ultimately humanistic end, and that he could see it as the only possible means just because there was not yet in the world anything that resembled a democratic liberal state.

I suggest that that prescription is not necessary now, and that if it can be discarded the chances of reaching Marx's humanistic goals are much brighter. This is so because the vanguard state or rule by a vanguard is simply inconsistent with participatory democracy, and it is inconsistent with the final goal. Of course Marx counted on the state withering away, but the 20th century record on that is certainly not reassuring. I hope I am not making the mistake that many social democrats, I think, make, namely, the mistake of thinking that everything can be left up to the present parliamentary institutions with their acknowledged bias against widespread participation in any political process. Marx was surely right in assuming that wide participation would be needed in order to replace capitalism and the capitalist state, and he was right in thinking that this participation must be a kind in which people begin to change themselves, begin to attain a new consciousness of their own possibilities.

Marx seemed to have expected that the very depth of working-class alienation would lead members of the class to the new consciousness of their own nature, a consciousness that would feed on and be fed by their own involvement in the revolutionary movement. But, as I have said, our working class isn't that revolutionary. It doesn't feel that alienated, which is why it seems to me we can't count on that. So the question is: what kinds of participation other than participation in a revolutionary worker's movement could possibly do the job? What could feed a new consciousness, turning away from consumerist satisfaction with simply material standards?

I've argued in one or two places that there are such kinds of participation now visibly emerging and likely to increase in strength and in potential as a leaven that could change the whole nature of the progressive movement. I mean movements concerned more with the quality of life than with the quantity of consumables. To mention only a few: the ecological movement, the anti-pollution movement, the related anti-nuclear and disarmament movements, various neighbourhood movements against the developers and against inner city decay, the movement for participation in the work place, worker's control or industrial democracy (certainly not much of that on this continent, but quite a bit of it in Europe) and, not least, the women's movement.

Well now, nobody knows if all these movements together can really be the steam of a movement which can transform capitalism. If they can, they would presumably be doing it without having to resort to vanguard rule, because all these movements get their steam from widespread grassroots participation. Incidentally,the whole process then wouldn't be relying on the working class entirely, because much of the steam for these movements comes from the middle class rather than or in addition to the working class.

F.C.   *Regarding vanguardism, some say that avoiding a vanguard movement is just not realistic. The change of consciousness to which you referred surely would be a long and painful one. It would also be subject to a variety of forms of distorted consciousness which could be taken advantage of by powerful enemies of socialism and humanism, and in this environment would there not be a necessity for a well-organized group of people simply to take charge, namely, a vanguard?*

C.B.M. In fact, I have been reproached with overlooking just such a danger quite recently. A paper presented by Professor John Seaman at the American Political Science Association Meeting in Denver in September in effect made much the same point you just made. Suppose this process of change of consciousness does get started from the grassroots and does begin to make the political process more responsive and more participatory; still, that is likely to take an awfully long time. So the political authority, no matter how democratic it is, is likely to feel the need to hurry it up. And that brings in a vanguard claiming to know our needs better than we do, and endangers the whole prospect of transition to a good society.

In reply I would say two things. First, although I have to agree there is a risk here, surely there is less risk to the whole transition prospect, and less risk to the achievement of basic human values in starting without a vanguard than if we were to put our reliance on a vanguard right from the beginning. Secondly, if what I consider the basic liberal and the basic Marxist value of individual self-development is not made the mainstay of the whole attempt at transition to a good society, then there won't be any transition; it won't even get started. And you can't make individual self-development a central value if you resign your judgment to a vanguard at the beginning. So on both those grounds I think the risk has to be discounted as less dangerous than the vanguard route.

F.C.   *Another challenge that must surely be met has to do with the proletariat. Could one not say in response to your comments on this subject that only the working class has sufficient power to secure or safeguard socialism, and therefore all other movements you mentioned must take second place?*

C.B.M.   I think it is simply not true, at least not in North America, that the working class is the only repository of this power. It has not used its power in the way socialists have wanted and shows very little sign of using its power to do this. It has used its power to get immediate material benefits or to hold on to its share but has not gone much beyond what Lenin called trade union consciousness, and I think that we cannot count on the traditional working class as an adequate resource. I don't think the working class on this continent is a force that is available for moving ahead to these ultimate goals, as contrasted with these other sorts of movements that I have just mentioned: the ecological movement; and anti-nuclear movement; workers' control movements where they exist (but they are a pretty late starter on this continent anyway); the peace movement; and the women's movement (and I know there is some criticism as well as a great deal of debate in women's circles and in Marxist circles about where the two should interact and how they could).

Because I don't think that the straight working class movement is itself an adequate available force for the transition, I think that all of these other movements together are much more likely to move us ahead now. It seems to me that it is quite wrong for Marxists to say none of these other movements must be allowed to get in our way, that they must all be treated as secondary, and that the great reliance must be placed on the working class movement in a very tightly controlled way. That is really just throwing away resources making for change in the right direction, resources that could not be used if they were all to be denied any support except insofar as they were a part of a strictly working class movement. After all, a lot of these other movements are propelled rather more by middle-class people than by the working class, so that to insist that the working class should not encourage all these others seems to me to be completely short-sighted. For one thing it is rejecting the use of all the non-Marxist women's energies, and really that's a case of a Marxist cutting off his nose—and it is "his" rather than "her" nose, I think—to spite his face.

F.C.   *Do you think that Marxism, itself, has anything to offer to the women's movement?*

C.B.M.   No doubt it has. But what worries me is the probability that the theorists of the women's movement who start from Marxist positions are apt to end up in a narrow position that logically they don't have to take, but it seems to me there is a danger that they would do so. I have just one other point about the role of the women's movement. I think that the large part of it that is middle-class rather than working-class ought to be fully utilized. Working-class women aren't a sufficient resource, for just the same reason that working-class men aren't. The working-class, both male and female, have to devote their efforts largely to maintaining their real material incomes, that is, maintaining their positions as consumers, and are not likely to get too far beyond that horizon, whereas the middle and professional classes, male and female, are not yet reduced to that dependence on that narrow horizon. They still have some energy to devote to pressing for the quality of life rather than just material quantity. It's important, I think, to tap a resource which is now becoming more and more one that can be used consistently with Marxism, because they are both ultimately concerned with the quality of human life.

F.C.   *Thank you very much.*

Notes

1. C. B. Macpherson, *The Real World of Democracy* (Toronto: Canadian Broadcasting Corporation, 1965); reprinted many times, most recently by Anasi Press (Concord, Ont., 1992). Macpherson's was the fourth in a still-ongoing series, named in honour of Vincent Massey, former Governor General of Canada. In this prestigious series, other lecturers have included Gregory Baum, Ursula Franklin, Northrop Frye, R. D. Laing, George Steiner, and Charles Taylor.
2. Crawford Brough Macpherson, *The Political Theory of Possessive Individualism* (Oxford: Oxford University Press, 1962).
3. C. B. Macpherson, *Democratic Theory: Essays in Retrieval* (Oxford: Oxford University Press, 1973).
4. *Ibid.*, 65–66.
5. C. B. Macpherson, "Liberal Democracy and Property," in C. B. Macpherson, ed., *Property: Mainstream and Critical Positions* (Toronto: University of Toronto Press, 1978), 199–297, and *The Rise and Fall of Economic Justice and Other Essays* (Oxford: Oxford University Press, 1985), essays 6 and 7.
6. Macpherson, *Democratic Theory*, essay 5.
7. This point is made by Joseph H. Carens in his introduction to a collection of essays based on a conference about Macpherson's thought, *Democracy and Possessive Individualism: The Intellectual Legacy of C. B. Macpherson* (New York: Routledge, 1993), though the relevant methodological categories Carens identifies only partially overlap with those discussed in this essay. Carens has in mind criticisms of Macpherson's historical scholarship by James Tully and criticisms of his inattention to institutional questions by Jane Mansbridge and John Keane in the volume he edited.
8. C. B. Macpherson, *The Life and Times of Liberal Democracy* (Oxford: Oxford University Press, 1977), chap. 1, 2–6. The "models" Macpherson explicates in this book are of democracy as "protective," "developmental," "equilibriating," and "participatory."
9. Ernesto Laclau, "The Signifiers of Democracy," in Carens, ed., *Democracy and Possessive Individualism*.
10. This is an important theme in Macpherson's *Democracy and Possessive Individualism*, the theoretical implications of which are several times returned to in his *Democratic Theory*.
11. The point is argued by Laclau in several places, including his *Hegemony and Socialist Strategy*, coauthored with Chantal Mouffe (London: Verso, 1985), see chap. 2.
12. An example is William Leiss in his monograph, *C. B. Macpherson: Dilemmas of Liberalism and Socialism* (Montreal: New World Perspectives, 1988) and in his

contribution to Carens, ed., *Democracy and Possessive Individualism*. Macpherson did not imagine, much less endorse, a deep ecological ethic or a hostile view toward science and technology. However, his views are compatible with recent critiques of consumerism and technologism, such as that by Andrew Feenberg (*Critical Theory of Technology* [Oxford: Oxford University Press, 1991], see especially the concluding chapter), and by Ursula Franklin, who named her 1989 Massey Lectures, "The Real World of Technology" (Toronto: CBC Enterprises, 1990), after Macpherson's earlier presentations.

13. Macpherson, *Democratic Theory*, essay 2, 24–25.

14. Demonstrating this was a major task of my *Democratic Theory and Socialism* (Cambridge: Cambridge University Press, 1987), chap. 6, in which references to several others defending the same claim are made.

15. The closest Macpherson comes to discussions of socialism *per se* are in his critique of Milton Friedman, *Democratic Theory*, essay 7, and in the essay, "Democracy, Utopian and Scientific," in *The Rise and Fall of Economic Justice*.

16. Macpherson's views escape the charge of class reductionism as I use this term in a treatment of this topic in *Democratic Theory and Socialism*, chap. 9.

17. The contributions of Connolly, Keane, Mansbridge, and Mouffe in Carens, ed., *Democracy and Possessive Individualism* take Macpherson to task on these issues.

18. Macpherson, *Democratic Theory*, 54–55.

19. The attempted retrieval of pluralism in *Democracy Theory and Socialism* is at 186–99, and the definition of ideal democracy to include negotiation is at 36–40.

20. *Ibid.*, 249–51 and 264–65.

21. Cautions qualifying his endorsement of the potential compatibility of vanguardism and democracy may be found in *The Real World of Democracy*, 19, and *Democratic Theory*, 106–7.

22. C. B. Macpherson, *Democracy in Alberta: Social Credit and the Party System* (Toronto: University of Toronto Press, 1953).

23. In a paper delivered at the 1979 meetings of the International Political Science Association in Moscow, reprinted in *The Rise and Fall of Economic Justice*, chap. 8. There Macpherson subsumed anarchist versions of communitarianism under "developmental individualism" and argued that capitalism inhibited each (pp. 94–96). Pluralism is referred to in passing in *Democratic Theory*, where Macpherson seems to have had the 1950s U.S. interest group theorists in mind, e.g., 201. In an essay written for *The Rise and Fall of Economic Justice*, published in 1985, entitled "Problems of Human Rights in the Late Twentieth Century," Macpherson anticipates more recent treatments of communities and individuals when in an aside he defends the collective rights of nations or aboriginal peoples on the grounds "that membership in a national or cultural community which has defined itself historically is part of what it means to be human, and is sometimes the most important part." Macpherson does not pursue this issue, but he predicts that: "We must soon rethink the dimensions of our cherished individualism" (23). See, too, Macpherson's exchange with the communitarian philosopher, Alasdair MacIntyre, *Canadian Journal of Philosophy*, Vol. 6, No. 2 (June 1976), 195–200, which reminded MacIntyre that possessive individualist society is partly to be criticized for its destruction of community.

24. Michael Walzer puts it that the philosopher should remain within Plato's cave, "Philosophy and Democracy," in John S. Nelson, ed., *What Should Philosophy Be*

Now? (Albany: State University of New York Press, 1983), 75–99.

25. Among other places, Nielsen defends this viewpoint in *Why Be Moral?* (Buffalo, NY: Prometheus Books, 1989), chap. 2.

26. Macpherson seldom addresses questions of ethical theory, and then only in passing. Thus in *Democratic Theory* he asks whether it is required to demonstrate the truth or falsity of postulates about the human essence, and concludes: "the truth or falsity of the postulate [about rejecting a possessive individualist view of human nature] is not in question. For it is not entirely a factual postulate. . . . It is an ontological postulate, and as such a value postulate" (37–38). In the ensuing pages it is not clear what theory about such values Macpherson has in mind, but in any case he is certainly not endorsing traditional ethical foundationism. In a similar vein, Macpherson criticizes ahistorical conceptions of needs in "Needs and Wants: An Ontological or Historical Problem," in Ross Fitzgerald, ed., *Human Needs and Politics* (New York: Pergamon Press, 1977), 26–35. And see Alkis Kontos, "Through a Glass Darkly: Ontology and False Needs," *Canadian Journal of Political and Social Theory*, Vol. 3, No. 1 (Winter 1979), 25–45, followed by a commentary by Macpherson.

27. Macpherson, *Democratic Theory*, 4.

28. Macpherson employs old-fashioned language in his list of truly human capacities, and he certainly located himself within a broadly humanist tradition. Thus, even though the historicist dimension of his thinking makes him less than a full-blown Enlightenment Rationalist, he still no doubt invites criticism from those who see sexist or culturally chauvinist bias in such a list. It should be noted, however, that the term "rational understanding" admits of several interpretations and that Macpherson includes reference to affective capacities.

29. "Scarcity was for millennia the general human condition; three centuries ago it became a contrived but useful goad; now it is dispensable. . . . We should say so. If we do not, the liberal-democratic heritage of Western society has a poor chance of survival" (*ibid.*, 38). Further to the question of ontology see note 26 above.

30. Macpherson, *The Real World of Democracy*, 67.

ESSAY 2

Democracy and Marxist Political Culture

This essay addresses Marxism neither as a body of texts nor as a set of theories deployed or attacked by professional historians, economists, and philosophers, but as a cultural phenomenon. In particular I wish to address the fact that whereas Marxism was once a central component of a democratic viewpoint toward the political world, it, like socialism, is now widely perceived as opposed to democracy. As I see it, the main contributions to democratic progress found in an earlier Marxist political culture and, of course, defended by Marx himself were the observation that such progress could be meagre at best in a world divided between capitalist exploiters and the people obliged to work for them and the concomitant vision of a postcapitalist world in which relatively equal distribution of the world's wealth ("to each according to need") removed one of the major impediments to full democratic participation.

Those who agree with these once widespread beliefs must consider it a tragedy of world historical proportions that capitalism has come to be associated with democracy and socialist equality with undemocracy in much contemporary popular thought and regard it as the order of the day for

Versions of this paper were read at the annual meetings of the Society for Socialist Studies, Victoria, B.C., May 1990, and at a conference on "Marxism in the 1990s" sponsored by the Bulgarian Institute of Philosophy in Varna, June 1990. It was published in the Socialist Studies Annual No. 7, Jos Roberts and Jesse Vorst, eds., *Socialism in Crisis?: Canadian Perspectives* (Winnipeg: Fernwood Publishing, 1992).

democratic socialists to retrieve a political culture wherein this name ("democratic socialism") is not considered a contradiction in terms. One is thus confronted with the enormous task of rebuilding a political culture in which key ideas associated with Marxism come once again to be generally regarded as integral to democracy.

The phrase "associated with Marxism" is employed to disavow any suggestion of special status for Marxist approaches to radical theory in respect of democracy. Also, the notion of rebuilding a political culture is taken as an alternative to the project of sifting through Marxist writings to prove that "true" Marxism has always been democratic. Rather, the propensity of Marxists to claim hegemonic status for a supposed flawless radical theory is regarded as part of the reason for the current contraposition of democracy and Marxism in popular political thought. While the political motivation of all the essays in this collection is to contribute toward the construction and promotion of a democratic-socialist culture, the present essay is specifically concerned to further this project by transcending both this propensity to heroize Marx and the analogous determination to vilify him. Instead, antidemocratic dimensions of a Marxist political culture will be identified and located as contradictory moments in the history of democratic theory and practice.

First, a limitation of speculative political-cultural, or indeed, any abstractly theoretical exercises for the purpose of democratic politics should be noted. Contemporary Marxists have proven themselves better at theorizing about the relation of theory to practice than at theorizing in a practical way. This requires striving to develop socialist and democratic theoretical hypotheses with explicit and informed reference to actual struggles. If I am not mistaken, this is exactly what Marx and Engels did in striving to integrate the democratic momentum of the French Revolution and the revolutions of 1848 with support for working-class struggles across national boundaries in Europe. Radicals should comport themselves in this same concretely practical manner, addressing themselves not just to struggles pertaining to conditions of work, but to the host of other focuses of struggle, all of which bear on both democracy and socialism.

In the common room of my own university philosophy department, for instance, I and my colleagues often participate in some lively discussions over ecological problems, special rights of native people in Canada or of the minority Quebec nation, the liberation of women, and so on. In these circumstances I note that we tend to take off our philosophical hats and to address the issues as if our philosophical orientations have little to do with these problems. I believe that, on the contrary, if progress is to be made in democratically motivated socialist theory, and hence to have any chance of affecting political culture, this will require allowing political-theoretical views to grow out of a process of directly confronting the many pressing matters of people's control over their lives, both in civil society and the state, that is, in matters of democracy. (The suggested approach is further explicated and illustrated in Essay 7.)

ANTIDEMOCRATIC DIMENSIONS OF MARXISM

Among the dimensions of a Marxist political culture—embraced, to be sure, not by all who have called themselves Marxists, but by enough to do harm—three seem to me paramount: First, the notion that the working class is the universal class, or that its objective interests represent the interests of all humanity in such a way that advancing what is taken as the cause of the working class should be the dominant or even exclusive concern of progressives. This viewpoint led to and reinforced a class-reductionist practice that divided democratic forces, detracted from discovering the origins and sustaining causes of such things as racism, national chauvinism, sexism, heterosexism, and so on, and it even contributed to the harbouring of such attitudes in the working class and elsewhere.

The second negative element I see in Marxist political culture is the idea that Marxism is a universal world view. A few years ago the (then) Italian Communist Party shocked the world of socialist orthodoxy (or rather accelerated its standing propensity to shock this world) by announcing that Marxism was no longer to be considered a world view, let alone one superior to other secular or even religious perspectives in virtue of which people give meaning to their lives. I believe that the Italian Communists were right to take this position. The unique contribution of Marxism is its critique of capitalism and capitalist-sustaining ideology. Also, being more concrete than other articulations of an egalitarian and communitarian moral vision,[1] it gives added force to this vision. These achievements do not require that, in addition, Marxism be a complete and synoptic world view. What is more, its pretense in this direction has created an ethic of intolerance or condescension toward non-Marxist perspectives that fosters antipluralist, antidemocratic practices and has facilitated statist assault on the traditions of civil society.

Finally, there is the notion of an epistemologically privileged vanguard. This negative component of Marxist political culture functions with the other two, as it is believed that those in full command of the Marxist world view are able to understand the objective interests of the working class and to help it to perform its world historical mission by acting for their true interests.

Aside from ignoring Marx's injunction that the educator be educated,[2] this orientation could only have encouraged and rationalized extreme paternalism—that is, acting against people's wishes in matters that affect them while claiming that this is for their own good.

Paternalism is bound to be antidemocratic insofar as democracy has to do with people participating in making a social environment conform to the wishes they actually have, not to those somebody else thinks they ought to have. And it is even more antidemocratic when combined with a pernicious "kinds of democracy" orientation—one distinguishing between what are called bourgeois and proletarian democracy—in accord with which the paternalist can pretend that in thwarting people's will one is in fact acting democratically, in a supposed superior sense of that word.[3] Since the claim to paternalistic authority is that the people do not know what is good for them, the paternalist always has a reason for blocking democratic access to decision making, and a downward spiral in democracy is created.

The Democratic Dialectics of Marxism

As to the analysis of these antidemocratic aspects of socialist political culture, no doubt several approaches are possible. The one I shall sketch strives to avoid moralistic condemnation of anyone who ever held or promoted any such attitudes, or attributing to them the harbouring of a bad philosophical theory or the like. Having myself once endorsed soft versions of the tenets criticized above, I am hardly in a position to adopt such a stance. More importantly, Marxist political culture, good and bad, like any cultural phenomenon, is too widespread to admit of a moralistic approach. Instead, I shall make use of the work of some contemporary democratic theorists to identify tensions and contradictions within democratic processes themselves which might give rise to the antidemocratic elements I claim to have identified.

Thus, one might understand the notion that the working class is universal by taking account of the fact that working-class struggle, like almost all large-scale democratic struggles, has taken place in a situation of adversity. In a world of class, national, racist, sexist, and other oppressions, democratic progress is seldom made positively, as it were, by just figuring out how to enhance the already secure level of collective self-determination enjoyed by a people; it is a negative and hard-fought struggle against powerfully entrenched opposition. The radical democratic theorists Ernesto Laclau and Chantal Mouffe argue that in such circumstances the identities of people in struggle are in part negatively defined in such a way as to promote sectarian and reductionistic attitudes by them toward others. As Laclau and Mouffe note, this is not unique to the working class, but seems to be a general phenomenon found as well in the women's movements or movements for national liberation, for example.[4] In each case it is an understandable tendency, which nonetheless needs constantly to be resisted.

An analysis of the tendency to make of Marxism a universal world view may also be approached in terms of the "dialectics of democracy" by extending a thesis of Claude Lefort concerning the negative effects of democratic revolutions. Referring specifically to the French Revolution, and attempting to take account of what he sees of value in conservative critiques of it, Lefort observes that in displacing traditional authority—the divinely sanctioned royal family—this revolution emptied the space of political power of anything concrete, leaving only the abstract notion of "the people." Since abstractions cannot govern, this space was occupied by the Jacobins, who, acting in the name of the people, were able to behave with antidemocratic excess without either traditional or popular constraint. Lefort extends this analysis to the Russian Revolution as well.[5]

Now, just as traditional agents of authority are displaced in democratic revolutions, so are traditionally sanctioned world views, thus creating an analogous void at the level of ideas. One might, then, speculate that the tendency to elevate Marxism to the level of a comprehensive and overriding world view was partly motivated and facilitated by this circumstance. To this extent there is some force to the challenge that Marxism had become a secular religion. (It is worth noting that bourgeois political cultures born of democratic revolutions do not escape this tendency either. It can be seen, for example, in the nationalistic jingoism that makes up a large part of French or United States popular political consciousness.)

Similar considerations apply to elitist vanguardism, but here I think an additional factor is at work, especially concerning Marxist intellectuals. Among the complexities that make democratic politics so difficult is that progress in democracy simultaneously requires both respect for the dominant values of a population and also critique of them. Critique is important partly to weed out antidemocratic beliefs and values that may nonetheless be popularly held (sexism and racism are obvious examples), and partly it is required so that people are not locked into set ways of thinking but can come to evaluate their own values, thus exercising control over themselves and not just over their surrounding environments. Cultural revolutions can be democratically pursued only if this ability exists and is itself valued.

Among the ways that societal critique takes place is by the work of professional critics within the intelligentsia. These people are those that Michael Walzer calls "the company of critics." He recounts the biographies of several people who were especially good at criticizing their societies while maintaining organic links with their dominant traditions.[6] These people are, however, rare in virtue of the extraordinary difficulty of this task, especially in those societies—that is, all of them—in which powerful vested interests are able to influence public opinion in a conservative way and where the conditions of life and work militate against critical thinking. This does not mean that the company of critics ceases to exist, but that it becomes too distanced from popular opinion to affect it. Hence the professional critic becomes alienated and frustrated. I speculate that in these situations a company of alienated Marxist critics finds the notion that it is part of an epistemologically privileged vanguard attractive.

This, then, is an outline of how the dialectics of democracy might help one understand antidemocratic components of Marxist political culture. Paradoxically, to the extent that the analysis succeeds, it underlines the *pro*democratic impetus of Marxism, even in its negative elements. On this view it is partly in virtue of participation in the democratic project that Marxism has come to exhibit these negative features. However, just noting this does not offer solutions. Some practical prescriptions follow directly and obviously from the analysis. The idea that the working class is the universal class should be given up, as should the pretense that Marxism is a general world view. One might think that vanguardism could be retained but be pursued nonpaternalistically. I do not think that this is desirable (or realistic, given its recent history), since vanguardism is inseparable from a paternalistic logic and is bound to lead to democratic regress.

An *anti*democrat might say that nothing is to be done and that what I call democracy's dialectics is really its impossibility. This challenge is most easily met on a conception of democracy not as something that a society either entirely possesses or entirely lacks, but as a process admitting of degree. In the 1950s, some liked to talk of a "technological fix" to describe what they saw as a potential in technology to correct any problems that it, itself, created, such as pollution or nuclear waste. This view was, of course, foolish, pernicious, and often self-serving, but on a degrees-of-democracy approach (along with certain empirical assumptions), an analogous concept of a *democratic* fix can be defended.[7]

The democrat need not deny that democracy creates problems. Rather, it needs to be insisted that problems caused by democracy be addressed by striving for *more democracy*. In particular, the sectarian propensities of people in struggle need to be addressed by constructing democratic habits of thought and action among those active in combatting a variety of oppressions. In place of trying to make Marxism or any other radical orientation the common world ideology, radicals should strive to defend a critical pluralism. The company of socialist critics should strive to reestablish links with the traditions of their populations, seeking out in the first instance whatever germs of prodemocracy can be found in them as starting places for their critical activity.

Subsequent essays will address some theoretical aspects of these recommendations, without denying their problematic natures. At the meeting of Canadian socialist scholars where an early version of this paper was read, it met strongly expressed resistance from two sources: those who thought it too soft on Marxism and those who regarded it as objectionably anti-Marxist. A thesis of the essay is that confrontation of the difficult tasks democratic socialists face requires avoiding both sorts of response.

Notes

1. Appropriate debates over whether or how Marxism can embrace a moral theory may be found in Kai Nielsen and Steven Patten, eds., *Marx and Morality*, *Canadian Journal of Philosophy*, Suppl. Vol. 7 (Guelph, Ont.: Canadian Association for Publishing in Philosophy, 1981).
2. Karl Marx, "3rd Thesis on Feuerbach," in *Karl Marx, Frederick Engels Collected Works*, Vol. 5 (New York: International Publishers, 1976), 3.
3. Much of the first part of my *Democratic Theory and Socialism* (Cambridge: Cambridge University Press, 1987) is devoted to a critique of approaches to democracy that divide it into kinds. See chap. 3.
4. Ernesto Laclau and Chantal Mouffe, *Hegemony and Socialist Strategy* (London: Verso, 1984), chap. 3; and see Laclau's *New Reflections on the Revolution of Our Time* (London: Verso, 1990), chap. 5.
5. Claude Lefort, *L'invention démocratique* (Paris: Fayard, 1981).
6. Michael Walzer, *The Company of Critics* (New York: Basic Books, 1988).
7. The thesis of the "democratic fix" is defended in my *Democratic Theory and Socialism*, chap. 4.

ESSAY 3

Democratic-Socialist Continua: Good and Bad

According to what might be called the continuity thesis among socialist theorists, democracy and socialism are inseparable. The dramatic destruction of most of the world's socialist governments in the name of democracy and with large-scale popular support clearly poses a problem for this thesis. With the exception of those relatively few who saw no grain at all of genuine socialism in the deposed regimes and of the surely even fewer who doggedly defend the erstwhile socialisms as being somehow truly democratic, democratic-socialist theorists are now obliged to rethink their subject. This essay's task is to indicate where key conceptual decisions must be made to clarify the relation of democracy to socialism and to show in what respects they are and are not continuous.

"DEMOCRACY"

Let us begin with "democracy," the word. In recent decades, debates among political theorists over what meaning to give this term have typically focused

This paper expands upon an article published in *Critica Marxista*, Vol. 27, No. 6 (November/December 1989). It has profited from comments by participants at a conference sponsored by the György Lukács Foundation and the journal *Eszmélet* in Budapest, April 1991. At that conference, which brought together editors of socialist journals "nonaligned" with political parties from North America, Western Europe, and Eastern Europe, participants were asked to offer capsule definitions of "socialism" and "democracy." Intrigued by the responses, I repeated this experiment later that year in China and in Cuba. The results are summarized in the appendix to this essay.

on so-called revisionist challenges to a classical concept of democracy as popular self-government. Theorists of the left have principally concerned themselves to defend this classical notion of popular sovereignty against recommendations of such as the economist Joseph Schumpeter or the political-scientific "realists" of the 1950s and 1960s that democracy be considered as no more than a means whereby elites can compete for political power or as institutional arrangements to regulate conflict among interest groups.

No doubt the revisionist conceptions describe part of the actual functioning of democratic politics in countries with parliamentary systems of government. However, it does not follow that this is *all* there is to democracy or that it *ought* to be exclusively regarded in these ways. In this essay I shall assume that defenders of the classical notion can meet revisionist attempts to redefine "democracy."[1] Instead, I shall address differences among classic and especially left democratic theorists sometimes obscured by their interest in combatting the revisionists. Of paramount importance is the question of whether there are kinds of democracy.

Kinds of Democracy

As is well known, Lenin argued in his polemic with Kautsky that one must never talk of democracy *per se*, but must always ask which class interests are served by a form of government called "democratic."[2] Generations of revolutionary socialists after Lenin have invoked this text to maintain that democracy is not a univocal concept, but should be class-relativized. In this tradition the term "democracy" has radically different senses in a bourgeois environment and a proletarian environment. The opinion that democracy thus admits of different kinds is not unique to Leninism, but is also advanced, for example, by anarchists and other champions of participatory democracy, who see "representative" and "direct" democracy as being incompatible. Alternatively, "democracy" is regarded univocally such that, for example, a capitalist and a socialist state may be compared on the basis of the common standard of democracy.

I take the choice between a univocal and a multivocal concept of democracy—indicated in Chart 3.1—as fundamental and argue that a realistic univocal conception is available and that the alternative approach is something to be avoided. In addition to denying one a standard by reference to which social or economic systems, modes of government, political cultures, or other things can be compared, the fragmentation of democracy into different kinds can be, and has been, antidemocratic. If the activities of authoritarian socialist state leaders have undemocratic consequences, this is too easily rationalized by maintaining that critics are thinking in terms of the *wrong kind* of democracy.

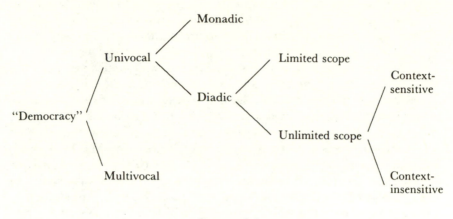

CHART 3.1

Degrees of Democratic Control

Similar to the choice of whether "democracy" is a univocal concept is that of whether it should be defined by reference to some property, for example, "according to majority vote," such that anything that has the property is democratic, and anything that lacks it is not. In contrast to this perspective, where something is either democratic or not democratic, one may think of democracy as admitting of degree. In the first case, the theorist will seek a monadic definition of the word "democracy"; in the second, it will be considered important to define the diadic relation "X is more democratic than Y," where X and Y range over the sorts of things thought capable of being more or less democratic. My principal reason for favouring the "degrees" approach is that it directs political theory and practice toward the task of making progress in democracy in one's own society, recognizing that it is always possible to increase its level of democracy (or indeed, to suffer regress in democracy by losing a level already achieved).

Crudely summarized, I think that democratic progress has been made when more people come to have effective control over a shared social environment than had previously been the case. On this formulation the object of democracy—what is taken to be more or less democratic—is the actual control[3] people exercise over a shared environment, thus implicating three related definitional features: (a) It is not sufficient, on this view, for people only to have a *chance* at control, for example, to be legally empowered to vote, since degrees of democracy are estimated by reference to success at control. (b) In particular, though usually democratic institutions are required for ongoing joint control of a shared environment, they are not part of the meaning of "democracy."[4] Participating in a wildcat strike or a mass demonstration may sometimes be democracy enhancing, while voting in a Tweedledee/Tweedledum election may not. And (c) though most efforts at shared control probably involve making collective decisions, this is regarded as more or less democratic in proportion to its likelihood of achieving actual control.

To be sure, these claims are contested, and perhaps a democratic theorist who otherwise agrees with the overall aims of this essay could achieve them, taking as the object of democracy "means of participation" (formal or otherwise) or "collective decision making." There are theoretical advantages and disadvantages to each definitional approach. However, in addition to solving some problems in social choice theory,[5] I favour an "actual control" approach, articulating, it seems to me, what it is about democracy in virtue of which people estimate the democratic potentials of alternative institutions or ways of making collective decisions.

A reason to start with actual control is that by identifying what democratic procedures and institutions are to accomplish, it helps to focus debate over the kinds of things needed to expand democracy. Thus in *Democratic Theory and Socialism* I asked whether shared control in the ideal case would require commonality of values or peaceful cohabitation of differences, and, concluding that it requires both, prescribed as a guideline that democratic institutions be sought that can keep open the possibility of either reaching consensus or negotiating a compromise depending on specific circumstances.[6]

Contextualized Democracy

A more politically radical resistance to a degrees-of-democracy conception is voiced by critics who do not wish to admit that governmental policies and other features of the societies they criticize contain any democracy at all. This objection can partly be met by noting that just as on the perspective I wish to defend any society will contain some degree of democracy, so will it contain some degree of *un*democracy, and hence the antidemocratic features of a regime can be acknowledged. However, to appreciate fully the advantages of a degrees-of-democracy approach, it is helpful to turn to the remaining choices marked in Chart 3.1. To think that democracy is of unlimited scope invites one to inquire into the level of democracy of any ongoing association of people—a country, a workplace, a church, a family, a university, a political party, a neighbourhood, and so on. This marks another difference from those classic conceptions that limit democracy to formal decision making in institutional, governmental situations. It also underlines a difference with revisionist approaches, all of which thus limit the scope of democracy.

Similarly, while major advances in democracy may be made on a society-wide scale, as for example in the case of successful national liberation struggles or political transformations such as the French Revolution, it is a mistake according to the degrees approach to think either that before these events there was no democracy at all or that further progress cannot be made after the events. To "contextualize" democracy, in the manner of Macpherson as discussed in the first essay, is to reject the notion that there are certain forms of government or manners of making collective choices that always achieve progress in democracy in any social setting. Rather, optimal means for making such progress will depend on a society's specific history and actual conditions.

THE VALUE OF DEMOCRACY

Turning now from the word "democracy" to democracy the thing (or rather the process), a conception generated by the choices summarized above invites one to suppose that no society, or part of a society, is ever completely lacking in democracy and that, taking levels of democracy already achieved (be they ever so slight), it is possible to achieve democratic progress, always

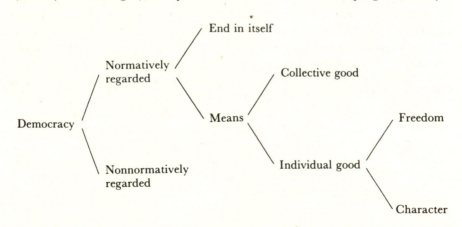

CHART 3.2

in society-specific ways. Since what is possible is not always desirable, some stance on the worth of democracy is required.

This conceptual map, like the previous one, is not meant to be exhaustive of all possibilities, but to indicate where I think four key decisions need to be made. Unlike the definitional map, none of these decisions is an exclusive one. Regarding the first decision, I believe it can be shown that, antidemo-crats of the left and the right to the contrary, one reason to favour more democracy is that this makes for efficiency, for instance in mobilizing a population to meet economic or other crises or in generating mutual feedback between administrators of policy and those affected by policy. Thus a case that does not appeal to what is morally desirable can be made for democracy, as has often been argued both by many Marxists and by non-Marxists of the revisionist school earlier referred to. The problem with an exclusively non-normative justification, however, is that, on the one hand, it encourages a power-political conception of democracy, which under the guise of value-free realism has more than once justified despotic abuse of political power, while, on the other hand, it distances one from the value-laden terrain of popular political culture.

Normativism

Some on the political left object to any normative orientation. On this view socialist normativism detracts from class struggle by encouraging activists unrealistically to think that radical social change can be accomplished by moral persuasion. The view is also sometimes still expressed that a norma-tive orientation in political activism will constrain activists, who might find themselves obliged to engage in activity that violates traditional moral norms.[7] It seems to me important to reject left-wing antinormativism and to argue instead that among the reasons to favour democracy are the morally desirable consequences of making progress in it.

Perhaps the left critics think a normative orientation involves elitist and didactic preaching or the construction of Rationalistic systems of ethics. The normative approach to democracy I have in mind, however, is closer to what Gramsci referred to when he insisted that revolutionaries must offer society values. Radical social transformation requires that radicals present their political project as being simultaneously the realization of the best of existing norms and the embodiment of a new vision, the attraction of which becomes a motivating aspect of common sense.

Democracy as a Means

Adopting a normative approach to democracy does not by itself address the grounds for favouring it, and here we confront another point at which a politically relevant choice must be made. Many democrats think that democracy should be valued as an end in itself.[8] Perhaps, given the right sort of ethical theory, a persuasive argument can be made to this effect, but it seems to me there are some reasons to resist it as a primary focus. One of these relates to context sensitivity. For democracy to be considered an end in itself, some way that people might collectively exercise control over a shared environment would have to be designated as the essence of democracy, which is to be valued for its own sake.

In addition to doubting that any one mode of shared control is ideally suited for all social contexts, I fear that this attitude may paradoxically have *anti*democratic consequences. In my experience it is most often expressed by democratic theorists who favour direct or participatory democracy in opposition to representative democracy and who think that full participation in achieving consensus is always superior to delegation of authority or negotiation from positions in conflict.[9] The result can too easily be that those not won over to consensus or those who wish to delegate some powers to representatives are excluded from democratic political processes.

Another reason to think of democracy as a means is to promote pluralism. A society is pluralistic to the extent that people in it are free to pursue their own concepts of the good life in their own ways. Social theorists in the Rousseauean tradition sometimes maintain that a society of complete harmony of interest is possible and desirable, just as some Marxists used to argue that in an advanced postcapitalist society, material superabundance would achieve the same harmonious effect. Supporters of democracy need not endorse either of these problematic claims, but can urge that the more democratic a society is, the less mutually threatening will be conflicts among its members. In this way democracy is compatible with pluralism. At the same time, insofar as democratic laws and procedures place constraints on complete freedom and often oblige compromise, there is also a tension between democracy and pluralism. This tension will be less severe when democratic politics are carried on with the explicit goal of promoting pluralism, that is, when pluralism is seen as an end of democracy.

Individuals and Collectives

Democracy might be thought to serve the "collective good" in one or more of three ways. Those in the Rousseauean tradition just mentioned sometimes think democracy valuable when it contributes to the construction of a cooperative spirit, a "general will" on one interpretation of this elusive term, where the collective is the entire society. Or, at a quite distant point on the political-theoretical spectrum, the neo-Hobbesian interest group theorists (who also call themselves "pluralists") take as the collective good group-specific interests. Finally, "communitarian" theorists address as their basic unit communities of people bound by common values embodied in the religious, class, national, or other traditions they share. I think it can be shown that democratic institutions, practices, and habits of thought do in fact serve *each* of these respective goods better than do alternatives, and this constitutes a reason to favour democracy. However, I do not think that this should be regarded as the most important reason.

One consideration in favour of taking individuals as more basic than collective goods insofar as justifying democracy is concerned is that even though individuals owe their characters and values to the social environments which create them, individuals are in one respect more complex than groups. Any individual is the product of a large number of different group-related conditions and of the historically specific character of their conjunctures. The result is that individuals' identities are always compound and changeable. Hence, one cannot identify the good of the individual with the good of any group of which he or she is a member.

No doubt somebody could grant this but claim that in the case of conflict, the needs of the group should take precedence over the needs of the individual. Among other things, this attitude is conceptually confused. Whatever social-theoretical stand one takes on the metaphysical status of group entities, it must be recognized that it is individuals and not social groups who actually experience the benefits of democracy or suffer the oppression of autocracy. Moreover, the experience of late socialism, where authoritarian oppression of individuals was for so long conducted in the name of the collective good, surely has shown the pernicious nature of this approach.

Character

One might try to have it both ways by arguing that democracy is justified *because* it molds the character of individuals, by making them responsible members of a political community.[10] This has long been a claim of democratic participationists. The complementary view that democracy *requires* a certain character to be ongoing also has a long heritage in civic republican-ism, recently revived by some theorists of the democratic left.[11] Without at all disagreeing with the claims about education and democracy or the impor-tance of building a character of civic responsibility, I wish to urge, none-theless, that democracy be justified primarily by reference to individual freedom, where "freedom" in this context is interpreted as the ability of people to act on their preferences.

Freedom

The unique virtue of democratic institutions and practices is that they increasingly enable people sharing a social environment to make that en-vironment conform to their wishes. Many left theorists strongly object to any such justification. That it centrally appeals to individuals is thought to reinforce a view of society as a forum within which asocial, atomistic indi-viduals compete for private accumulation: the possessive individualism com-batted by Macpherson. Conceiving of freedom as satisfaction of present preferences is thought to ignore the way preferences are socially formed and capable of manipulation.

These are, indeed, weighty considerations. Against them is the concern that justification of democracy by reference to something other than its potential to extend freedom in this narrow sense—or, what comes to the same thing, an alternative conception of "freedom"—cannot avoid sanctioning action against people's wishes on the putative basis that this is for their own good, that is, paternalism. As insisted upon in Essays 1 and 2, such institutionalized paternal-ism was at the heart of authoritarian socialism, where it generated a downward, antidemocratic spiral and was especially insidious since paternalists could pre-tend to others, and maybe even to themselves, that in acting against popular will they were in fact acting democratically.

Moreover, adopting such a viewpoint on the justification of democracy does not preclude viewing individuals as socially formed, since what is at issue is how best, in situations where control of a common environment may be shared, to satisfy people's aspirations, not how they come to have the aspirations they do.[12] Nor does it make freedom in this sense the highest value. To anticipate a point to be developed in the discussion of socialism below, there is nothing in this conception to prevent debate over what people *ought* to prefer. The question for the democrat, as I see it, is rather whether such debate is best pursued in a situation where, as far as possible, joint determination of a shared environment is made in accord with the prefer-ences people actually have or in accord with those some parties to the debate think they ought to have. The latter situation is nothing but paternalism.

The Democratic Fix

As to ferreting out and combatting manipulated preferences, building character, and promoting civic republicanism, of course all these are important for a robust democracy. If democracy were viewed as an all-or-nothing affair, then, to the extent that these things are required for it, paternalism would necessarily precede democracy, thus creating a dilemma. However, on the conception of democracy employed here, democratic processes can move, spiral-like, in either an upward or a downward direction. This makes germane the thesis of participatory democrats that democracy has the potential to be self-educating. Impediments to democracy, including those created by democratic politics itself, are best addressed by *expanding* democracy.

On this thesis, one reason that people are prone to resolve conflict by force or to harbour antisocial values is that they have had insufficient experience in ongoing, collective decision making either to trust democratic procedures as reliable ways to achieve their various goals or to acquire habits of mutual respect and tolerance for others. The solution is not to despair of democracy, but to broaden and deepen it. In Essay 2, the assumption behind this policy was labelled by contrasting it with the once-popular notion of a "technological fix." Unlike this technocratic assumption, whereby problems created by technology were supposed to be solved by the application of more technology, a concept of the "democratic fix" can be defended, by which impediments to the ability of democratic practice to promote individual freedom are best addressed by more democracy.

SOCIALISM

Socialism as a concept is no less problematic today than what we have experienced of socialism as a reality. I am thinking not only of the mystifying notion of the dictatorship of the proletariat, but also of social democracy, which, like the Second International theory and practice it opposed, uneasily rides a contradiction between being the political arm of organized labour, on the one hand, and a voice of the population as a whole, on the other.[13] Recognizing that summary distinctions, like those above about democracy, do not fully capture such contradictions or other complexities of social and political reality, I nonetheless suggest that one begin by considering the widely held conceptions illustrated in Chart 3.3.

I am disinclined to engage in either textual or historical analysis of the use of these concepts, though the next essay will divide the terrain in a rather less pedagogical manner in order to explain politically significant confusions in classic texts. These concepts are selected because they are core ideas around

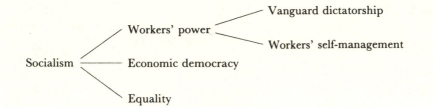

CHART 3.3

which socialist theory and practice is typically made sense of within the political culture of the left: Socialism as workers' power is the organization of political and economic structures to serve what are taken as working-class interests; a society exhibits economic democracy if decisions about production and distribution are democratically made; a socialist society is one the economy of which is structured to approximate equality. (Essays 4, 5, and 7 will argue in favour of socialism as equality of certain material benefits and burdens.)

The conceptions of Chart 3.3 can be combined, but more often they are simply confused in ways that preclude addressing some important problems. Thus, workers' power is sometimes equated, both by advocates of vanguard dictatorship and of workers' self-management, with economic democracy. But these are clearly different things, since a populace includes more than workers; and in any case, as we now well know, even workers might massively vote against what advocates of workers' power take to be in their proper interests. Similarly, material equality is sometimes advanced as an expression or form of economic democracy, but this cannot be the case, since, again, people might reject egalitarianism, or equality could be dictatorially imposed.

The Dictatorship of the Proletariat

Before proceeding, it will be best to put aside that conception of the dictatorship of the proletariat wherein socialism and democracy are thought radically *discontinuous* on class-relativized, power-political grounds. According to this view, democracy (no matter how conceptualized) is one of several tools that might be employed to further the more important end of working-class power, but one that is dispensable when it does not serve this end. I take this amoral, historicist conception of socialism to be a dangerous mystification, which has rationalized the most brutal expressions of authoritarian socialism. No matter what the setbacks for the socialist ideal recent reactions in Eastern Europe may represent, the experience will nonetheless have been enormously democratically progressive in my view if only the theory and the practice of this way of thinking have finally been put to rest.

Strong and Weak Continuity

Addressing, then, those who wish to maintain some continuity between socialism and democracy, one might first observe that on each conception, socialism may be thought continuous with democracy in either a strong or a weak way. Combined with a theory about democracy being divisible into kinds, the notion of the dictatorship of the proletariat is strongly continuous with democracy when it is thought to embody a special, higher form of democracy—one, as Lenin put it, "a million times more democratic than the most democratic bourgeois republic."[14]

On a weaker interpretation, the dictatorship of the proletariat is advocated as a benevolent authoritarianism, which, however, is supposed to result in full democracy when the dictatorship autodestructs. Socialism is considered strongly continuous with democracy on the remaining conceptions if it is thought that economic democracy or material equality will necessarily bring in their wake full democracy. They are weakly continuous if economic democracy and material equality are regarded as necessary but not sufficient for full democracy, or as I prefer to put it, for making major democratic progress.

We now have two senses of democratic-socialist continuity that I shall label "good," and one that will be called "bad." Against radical discontinuists, democracy and socialism are seen as continuous if the socialist project is subsumed within the democratic project, that is, if, as was well articulated by Macpherson and is echoed in the many recent writings of democratic socialists today, a principal reason to favour socialism is as a means for expanding democracy in large social units.

As between strong and weak senses of "continuity," I believe that any pretence to a strong link must be viewed with suspicion. If democracy is regarded as a matter of pervasive, complex, and reversible processes, then it would be most strange if there were a single sort of measure that could guarantee major and secure general progress in it. Perhaps the contrary opinion derives from an overly optimistic viewpoint associated with democratic revolutions like those of 1776, 1789, or 1848. That these achieved major democratic advances in certain domains of human life there can be no doubt, but few democratic theorists today, and none on the left, see them as guarantors of all the democracy that is desirable or attainable. Nor can many such theorists still have illusions about socialist revolutions; and the democratic revolutions of 1989 that deposed authoritarian socialism are now appearing to be similarly mixed bags.

Further, I believe that both strong and weak claims to democratic-socialist continuity within the conception of socialism as vanguard dictatorship should be avoided. This follows from considerations already advanced about democracy. In addition to other problems, the strong concept problematically fragments democracy into kinds, and the weak concept is at least paternalistic. Moreover, here we need not speculate, having witnessed the deep downward spiral of a socialism largely structured and justified according to the paternalistic model. It is for these reasons that the notion of socialism as the dictatorship of the proletariat should be rejected by a democratic socialist.

An advantage of subordinating socialism to democracy is that on the resulting perspective it is not pressing categorically to identify something as entirely socialist or entirely nonsocialist. Just as democracy is a complex matter of degree, so is socialism. Thus, if workers' power is dissociated from the idea, central to its articulation in terms of the dictatorship of the proletariat, that the working class somehow represents the universal interests of humanity, what remains are specifically working-class movements, such as trade unions or organizations of the unemployed, among whose activists are those who, like their politically oriented counterparts in other social movements, recognize the need to secure influence over or in the state.

One relatively narrow but historically sanctioned sense of "socialism" is, then, movement politics addressing specifically working-class oppression. Similarly sanctioned, especially in the tradition of social democracy, is the notion of socialism as democratic regulation of macroeconomic matters, and one might add to this generic concept workplace democracy, including, at a strong limit, workers' self-management (which accordingly could be located on Chart 3.3 as a form of economic democracy as well as of workers' power).

Now, if democracy involves people having effective control over important aspects of their lives, combatting working-class oppression or promoting economic democracy would constitute democratic gain (at least in the short term) in respect to these things. Whether it would contribute to the long-term expansion of society-wide democracy depends, in the case of working-class politics, on the extent to which sectarianism and hostility to other social movements could be overcome and, in the case of economic democracy, on the content of the economic policies a democratically empowered populace actually makes. It is partly for this reason that I favour classifying radical working-class politics and economic democracy with, respectively, means for achieving socialism and socialist institutional arrangements, reserving pride of place for the third historically entrenched concept of socialism—

equality—regarded as the ideal of socialism. It is in order to secure a society structured to certain measures and kinds of equality that appropriate means and institutional arrangements should be sought.

Equality

The concept of socialist egalitarianism I have in mind is a modest one. This means, in the first instance, that it does not involve levelling or the obliteration of difference, and it does not even prescribe that equality is always desirable. Rather, socialist egalitarianism as I interpret it *presumptively* prescribes equalization of the balance among a range of benefits and burdens. Taking the *balance* of benefits and burdens as that which is to be equalized allows one to conceive of things like acquiring a socially required skill as a burden or performing easy work as a benefit.

Including the notion of presumption sanctions deviation from strict equality when this is required to promote economic efficiency, to reward or encourage special effort, or to avoid antidemocratic threats. This list of possible grounds for limiting equality will be recognized as those typically given by procapitalists. The proper socialist response is to agree that these are legitimate kinds of grounds, while at the same time challenging procapitalist empirical assumptions or self-serving conceptions of terms like "efficiency" or "democracy" with reference to specific cases.

The approach adopted here is also modest with respect to complex and problematic questions about how to specify just what measures and kinds of equality should and can be championed by socialists. Insisting that the ideal of socialism include the notion of political equality is a species of the effort to make socialism definitionally democratic and is accordingly resisted in the modest conception. Rather, socialist equality is here regarded more narrowly as *material* equality and seen, like democracy, not as an end in itself, but as a (necessary though not sufficient) means to other things. This orientation, which is defended in Essay 4, is in keeping with the observation of one socialist theorist, Michael Luntley, that socialism "is not a moral theory which offers a particular vision of the good life, instead it is a theory about how the good life is possible."[15]

Modesty is not magic, however, and since conceptions of the good life notoriously differ, this approach removes a burden from specifically socialist theory without making it disappear. One reason to subordinate socialism to the political project of expanding democracy is scepticism about whether questions of what constitutes a good life can be answered (and, even if somehow proven, universally "sold") by philosophers. By contrast, it is a virtue of well-conducted democratic politics that it can, at least sometimes, find ways to enable people with alternative visions of the good to coexist and even mutually to enrich one another's perspectives. I take the evident current failures of such pluralism in previously socialist countries to derive in part from the paucity of practice in democratic politics suffered by their populaces under authoritarian rule.

This is not to claim that socialists or democrats can or should shun the grand philosophical questions. (In Essay 5, an approach is sketched to tensions between democratic politics and philosophy, and principles for addressing these tensions are suggested.) Nor is it denied that there are some philosophical questions internal to a conception of material egalitarianism. One of these is to decide whether and how benefits and burdens should be regarded subjectively, as preference satisfaction, or in some more objective way, for instance, as happiness or the realization of worthy potentials. Another question is whether what should be (presumptively) equalized are opportunities to achieve something or actual achievements. Whatever combination of choices one makes has both advantages and disadvantages, well illustrated in ongoing debates among philosophers of equality.[16]

Confining itself just to equality as a socialist ideal, this book suggests making a generic conception of material equality more precise by articulating both a *reactive* dimension of the notion, where socialist equality is regarded as the provision of material requirements for combatting systematic oppression (this is the main focus of Essay 4), and a *proactive* concept, where socialism aims to provide opportunities and capacities for people to pursue meaningful lives as they see them (Essay 8). On these views, socialist equality is something more than formal equality of opportunity, but less than full equality of results. The conceptions include some objective parameters, since, arguably, some conceptions of a meaningful life (one thinks of the National Socialists) should not be facilitated on moral grounds, and systematic thwarting of people who try to act on pernicious preferences should therefore not be considered oppressive. Also, it is a matter of objective judgment just what is required to overcome oppression or to pursue a meaningful life.

At the same time, to avoid paternalism, it is the thwarting of people's actual preferences (as opposed to objective interests or the like) that is central to identifying oppression, and a plurality of perceived ways to lead a meaningful life is allowed. This means that unless an implausible social or historical metaphysics is counted on to ensure that people's various counter-oppressive preferences and life plans mesh, the possibility of conflict among these things remains. There are clearly limits to how far philosophy can effectively address this situation. It is thus a political claim that increasing success in achieving socialist equality will permit one to confront resulting conflicts in increasingly felicitous and democratic ways.

Equality and Democracy

It was mentioned earlier that equality and democracy are continuous only in a weak sense. This is not just because equality only facilitates and does not necessitate democratic progress, but also because egalitarian structuring of a society has well-known antidemocratic potentials: Even the most flexible egalitarian structures require a measure of centralized planning, which in turn risks creating antidemocratic phenomena such as bureaucratization and invites state effort to force or to brainwash people to adapt their preferences to a plan. It is certainly because the antidemocratic potentials of equality outweighed its democratic ones, and indeed subverted equality itself by creating corruption and unjustified privilege in authoritarian socialism, that nearly all the prodemocrats from Eastern Europe I have talked with in recent years have considered egalitarianism at best naive.

Contrary to this opinion, however, I think it all the more important at the present time for socialists to regain the egalitarian ideal by exposing and combatting the antidemocratic effects of capitalist (as well as of socialist-bureaucratic) inequalities and by pressing for egalitarian measures far beyond those that are acceptable to large-scale capitalism. The task may not be as daunting as it seems. It is eased by growing popular concern about the social effects of pervasive poverty in industrialized countries and ecological and other problems generated by North/South economic disparities.

Affirmative Action

Also favouring the task is an additional "good" sense in which socialism and democracy are continuous, namely, that material equality participates in the democratic fix. That is, democracy and equality in principle form a mutually self-building process. For example, an affirmative action programme to increase the proportion of members of a society from systemically disadvantaged groups (in my country, women, visible minorities, native people, and the handicapped) in desirable jobs or government positions is simultaneously a democratic and an egalitarian effort, since such positions are both empowering and economically rewarding.

The intent of such programmes is increasingly to weaken systemic discrimination, with its inegalitarian and undemocratic consequences. That the programmes sometimes have divisive and even counterproductive effects is without question; however, these can be ameliorated to the extent that they are products of democratic debate and decision, rather than being imposed by a government agency, and to the extent that they are supplemented by employment support for members of nontargeted groups, who otherwise are economically threatened by affirmative action.

Markets

Another example may be especially germane to the rapid process of marketization now being undertaken in Eastern Europe and the former Soviet Union. I find three sorts of arguments for a market: (a) markets are needed to encourage incentive; (b) the democrat must recognize that many consumers and prospective producers and distributors *want* there to be a market; (c) the market is both the most efficient and the most democratic way to ascertain certain categories of consumer wants. Of these I consider (c) the most compelling. The second argument is, of course, one that formerly existing socialism was obliged increasingly to recognize. Procapitalists applaud popular demand for marketization as proof, with respect to argument (a), that only the promise of personal gain can generate innovation and the exertion of enterprising effort. On a democratic-socialist perspective, (a) and to a certain extent (b) are unfortunate products of decades of authoritarianism.

This opinion rests on the hypothesis that the economic and democratic benefits of markets can be secured in a mixed market/nonmarket economy without catering to or creating a culture of possessive individualism. In Macpherson's terms, as discussed in Essay 1, this requires integrating elements of a market *economy* with a nonmarket *society*. But this is possible only if egalitarian measures are maintained to prevent people from falling into economic despair (the fear of which leads them to accept demeaning and authoritarian working conditions or, alternatively, to engage in Hobbesian warfare) *and* if economic policy and other major decisions are made far more democratically than in authoritarian socialism or in contemporary capitalism. This assumes that currently narrow self-interest and consumerism take the place of that level of democracy necessary for people to feel a commitment to each other and to the future of their societies. I realize that simultaneous pursuit of such egalitarian and democratic politics is difficult, but invite critics to offer a less problematic alternative.

Democratic-Socialist Politics

The general point being made regarding this version of democratic-socialist continuity is that relative material equality frees people for meaningful participation in democratic activities, and that popular democratic involvement in the formation and implementation of equality-promoting policies generates commitment to them. If either democracy or equality were an all-or-nothing state of affairs, then a democratic-egalitarian fix would clearly be impossible. But if each is a matter of degree, then one can envisage a politics that seeks, in the fashion urged by Macpherson, to retrieve whatever exists in one's society of democratic and egalitarian values and practices and vigorously strives, in whatever ways are both appropriate given local circumstances and not subversive of the project itself, to promote their interactive expansion.[17] Such politics I call "democratic-socialist."

APPENDIX

Socialist Towers of Babel

The following definitions were solicited in the spring of 1991. In each case, participants were asked to imagine that they were granted a thirty-second "spot" on radio or television as experts. Several refused to respond due to the brevity constraint and because they—correctly—feared that the results might sometime find their way into print. Since in each forum there were groups of nearly synonymous definitions, slightly edited versions of the most succinct of each group are reproduced as samples. The definitions are listed in order of descending numbers of respondents giving versions of them.

DEFINITIONS OF "SOCIALISM"

BUDAPEST

(A conference of editors of socialist journals, nonaligned to political parties, from Eastern Europe, Western Europe, and North America, April.)

1. Social control of property relations.
2. Material and cultural equality.
3. Anticapitalist movement for a humanistic society.
4. The stateless self-organization of society (same as democracy).
5. Self-organization of citizens in defence against bureaucracy.
6. Swinging with your soul (*Mit der Seele baumeln,* from a German Socialist song).

HAVANA

(A conference of North American and Cuban philosophers, June.)

Cubans' Definitions

1. A social system that guarantees social justice and the dignity of the individual.
2. The conditions for democracy: the right to work, to health care, to education, etc.

3. The right to exist for one's self and others as a human, not as a statistic.
4. The conditions for humanizing man.

North Americans' Definitions

1. A system of government and of the distribution of the necessities of life for human development which guarantees that all in society receive the basic necessities needed to develop into a full human being.
2. Distribution of resources on the basis of need.
3. Social control of the economy.
4. Collective decision making in the governance of common affairs based on social ownership of social means of production.

DEFINITIONS OF "DEMOCRACY"

BUDAPEST

1. Equal participation of individuals simultaneously to pursue their unique and their shared interests.
2. The means to socialism.
3. No meaning at all.
4. A system to ensure that people do not get a better government than they deserve. [Taken from George Bernard Shaw.]

HAVANA

Cubans' Definitions

1. A form of the state to exert political power of the dominant class.
2. The established form by which man realizes his nature as a social individual in agreement with his surrounding society while progressively advancing to spiritual and material realization.
3. A form of expression of the socialist state; the right to participate in all spheres of its social order.

North Americans' Definitions

1. A system of government of an institution based on full participation of those affected by it, limited by guaranteed rights of all to such freedoms as of speech, life, etc.
2. Equal social decision making by all.
3. Government informed by popular power.
4. Collective decision making in the governance of common affairs.

LANZHOU (PRC)

(A course on democratic theory for senior students and professors of philosophy, April/May. Only definitions of "democracy" were solicited.)

1. A means to social stability whereby rulers use the people's will to maintain their domination.
2. Politics to enable citizens effectively to shape and organize their lives.
3. The distribution of goods, offices, powers, rights, and duties to the benefit of the majority.
4. The majority's autocracy (Mao).
5. Self-government of the people.
6. Many people eat the same apple in different ways and one person eats many apples the same way.

Notes

1. C. B. Macpherson defends his version of classical democracy ("developmental democracy") against Schumpeter's view in *The Life and Times of Liberal Democracy* (Oxford: Oxford University Press, 1977), chap. 4.
2. V. I. Lenin, *The Proletarian Revolution and the Renegade Kautsky, Collected Works*, Vol. 28 (Moscow: Progress Publishers, 1963–80), 226–325.
3. The term "control" is likely the key one for any classical approach to democracy, as it is by reference to it that such terms as "shared control" and hence "participation" are also given sense. I thus labour the definition of the term in *Democratic Theory and Socialism* (Cambridge: Cambridge University Press, 1987), 27–32, 301n.3, 302n.6. In general, I found the term "more democratic" difficult to define, and was not aided by the hundreds of definitions of "democracy" in political-theoretical literature, most of which are ideological in a pejorative sense. The full definition of the term occupies many pages of text and endnotes in the earlier book, see chap. 3.
4. This approach thus diverges from that of Brian Barry: "eighteenth-century England has been described as 'oligarchy tempered by riot.' But however efficacious the rioters might be, I would not say their ability to coerce the government constituted a democratic procedure." *Democracy and Power: Essays in Political Theory 1* (Oxford: Clarendon Press, 1992), 26. Barry's view recalls the observation that, like suicide, social revolution is only illegal if it fails. It is no doubt true that in large-scale social settings, the rule of law is, other things being equal, conducive to democracy; but it would be odd to say that violation of antidemocratic law in a way that expanded democracy is undemocratic until after its success. Also, for those who see democracy as of indefinite scope, there will be many social settings (neighbourhoods, families, classrooms, congregations, work collectives,

social circles, and so on) that might be more or less democratic, though formal procedures are inappropriate.

5. In particular, if "collective decision" is taken to be a primitive term, then the "paradoxes" identified by J. Kenneth Arrow and other social decision theorists become very difficult to escape. See Cunningham, *Democratic Theory*, 62–64.

6. *Ibid.*, 37–40.

7. See, for example, Richard Miller, *Analyzing Marx* (Princeton, NJ: Princeton University Press, 1984), 30ff.

8. For example, Seymour Martin Lipset: "Democracy is not only or even primarily a means through which different groups can attain their ends or seek the good of society; it is the good society itself in operation," *Political Man* (Garden City, NY: Doubleday, 1960), 403.

9. Examples are Jane Mansbridge, *Beyond Adversary Democracy* (New York: Basic Books, 1980), and Benjamin Barber, *Strong Democracy* (Berkeley: University of California Press, 1984).

10. A defence of this view is by William N. Nelson, *On Justifying Democracy* (London: Routledge & Kegan Paul, 1980).

11. Integrating civic republicanism with pluralist democracy has been a major effort of the democratic theorist Chantal Mouffe. See her introduction and contribution to the useful collection of essays organized around this theme, *Dimensions of Radical Democracy: Pluralism, Citizenship, Community* (London: Verso, 1992).

12. Marx's comment in his famous "6th Thesis on Feuerbach" that "the essence of man" is "the ensemble of the social relations"—*Karl Marx, Frederick Engels Collected Works*, Vol. 5 (New York: International Publishers, 1976), 4—is often referred to by radical theorists as support for their view that normative radical theory ought not to focus on individuals. For a criticism of the general position see Andrew Levine, Elliot Sober, and Erik Olin Wright, "Marxism and Methodological Individualism," *New Left Review*, No. 163 (March/April 1987). I discuss the point with specific reference to the 6th Thesis in "Community, Tradition, and the 6th Thesis on Feuerbach," in Robert Ware and Kai Nielsen, eds., *Analyzing Marxism, Canadian Journal of Philosophy*, Suppl. Vol. 15, 205–30.

13. Adam Przeworski describes this tension in *Capitalism and Social Democracy* (London: Cambridge University Press, 1985), see the chapter, "Social Democracy as an Historical Phenomenon."

14. Lenin, *Proletarian Revolution*, 248.

15. Michael Luntley, *The Meaning of Socialism* (La Salle, IL: Open Court, 1990), 14.

16. The principal philosophers addressing this topic include Ronald Dworkin, Michael Walzer, Amartya Sen, Tim Scanlon, Richard Arneson, Joshua Cohen, Thomas Nagel, and G. A. Cohen. Some recent articles are in *Ethics*, Vol. 99, No. 4 (July 1989), which includes a good survey of pertinent literature by G. A. Cohen, "On the Currency of Egalitarian Justice," 906–44. See, too, Kai Nielsen's socialist application of egalitarian theory in his *Equality and Liberty: A Defense of Radical Egalitarianism* (Totowa, NJ: Rowman & Allanheld, 1985), and the annotated bibliography by Louise Marcil-Lacoste, *La thématique contemporaine de l'égalité: Répetoire, résumés, typologie* (Montréal: Les Presses de l'Université de Montréal, 1984).

17. C. B. Macpherson, *The Life and Times of Liberal Democracy* (Oxford: Oxford University Press, 1977), 100–107.

ESSAY 4

The Critique of the Gotha Programme *Again: On the Relation between Socialism and Equality*

Egalitarian socialists cannot but find it ironic, indeed bitterly ironic, that after decades of condemnation by defenders of the late socialist states for a so-called bourgeois focus on equality (rather than on proletarian dictatorship), it is now egalitarian policies that are claimed to be proven hopelessly inefficient and antidemocratic by the fall of those very states.

Without exception, socialists who levelled the "bourgeois egalitarian" charge appealed to Marx's critique of the programme of the Lassallean wing of the Socialist Workers' Party founded in 1875 at Gotha. (The congress there united followers of the by-then-deceased Ferdinand Lassalle with those of Marx, August Bebel, and Wilhelm Liebknecht.) Whether the resulting union was a doomed attempt to mix oil and water is a fine historical question, the approach to which no doubt partly depends on one's stance toward matters of political theory raised by Marx in his critique and pursued in this essay.

A French-language version of this paper is forthcoming in the *Cahiers de recherche éthique*, special collection on equality. Thanks are due to Arthur Ripstein and Wayne Sumner for comments on earlier drafts. I have also profited from discussions about central aspects of the paper with Jacques Texier and Mario Reale. The main ideas expressed in it were formulated while teaching a course on equality with Louise Marcil at the Universities of Montreal and Toronto in the spring of 1990. I am grateful for contributions by her and by our students.

The intent of the essay, however, is not historical but forward looking, and Marx's *Critique of the Gotha Programme* is taken as a point of departure because, together with conflicting twentieth-century interpretations of its meaning, this document highlights the complexity of the theoretical task of relating socialism to equality and because the events around 1989 call for reassessment of the traditional intrasocialist debates on this topic, to which Marx's *Critique* has been central. One can begin by asking whether Marx was a pro- or an antiegalitarian. Marx refers to programmatic prescriptions favouring "equal right" or "fair distribution" as ideas which "have now become obsolete verbal rubbish," insisting that "it was in general a mistake to make a fuss about so-called *distribution* and put the principal stress on it." This denunciation, however, immediately follows his famous description of communist society: "From each according to his ability, to each according to his needs."[1]

Several commentators, as for example Etienne Balibar in his 1976 study of the concept of the dictatorship of the proletariat,[2] strive to make these passages consistent by stressing the transitional role Marx assigned socialism, a working-class state, in making possible a stateless communist society. In the former, bourgeois institutions and attitudes based on abstract concepts of individual rights are dismantled even while dialectically adopting distributional policies that embody a typical bourgeois principle of fair exchange of labour for pay: From each according to ability, to each according to work. By contrast, the needs-adjusted distribution of a projected communism will represent an egalitarian advance on the formal equality characteristic of the more democratic capitalist states. In more recent analyses (including by Balibar himself),[3] each dimension of this argument is challenged.

Kai Nielsen interprets Marx's disparaging remarks about distribution not as a normative rejection of equal distribution of wages for equal contributions of work, but as a distributional principle of (precommunist) socialism "circumscribed by determinate historical possibilities" and subject to morally progressive improvement with the new possibilities afforded by communism.[4] Jacques Texier maintains that the goal of advanced communism is neither formal nor substantive equality but the overcoming of inequalities and other constraints that impede the free development of each individual.[5]

Texier and Nielsen see a moral dimension in Marx's arguments, thus disagreeing with more power-political interpretations, and compared to the mountain of recent literature on the subject, little attention is devoted in their work to the precise nature of a supposed theory of (or against) justice on Marx's part.[6] (Though presented as commentaries, one has the impression that many of these debates are oblique efforts by the commentators to articulate their own views about justice and socialism.) The variety of positions in all such research generates a long list of permutations of elements of a Marxist theory about equality, and textual debates achieve sophistication of Talmudic proportions.

Begging leave to avoid joining these textual interpretive debates, let me now summarize a position—borrowing from Balibar, Nielsen, and Texier— that I take to be Marx's, or at least a common Marxist, orientation that makes the two passages earlier quoted from the *Critique of the Gotha Programme* cohere. The orientation is comprised of three core elements: a critique of equality in advanced capitalist society as no more than the possession by individuals of formal rights; the depiction of a postclass (communist) society in which needs-adjusted material equality and meaningful life and work have been achieved; and the claim that such a society requires a preparatory period (socialism, also called the "first phase of communism" by Marx)[7] during which period state power and the economy are under working-class control.

The sorts and extents of equality both possible and generally thought desirable in each of capitalism, socialism, and communism are conditioned by their respective production relations, which again are conditioned by the levels of their forces of production, where "conditioning" may be more or less strongly interpreted depending on how deterministic one thinks Marx's historical theory was. In socialism and communism, unlike capitalism, the means of production are cooperatively controlled. The Lassalleans are criticized for failing to distinguish between socialism and communism, for viewing socialism as a matter of "state aid"[8] rather than as working-class dictatorship, and for infusing a bourgeois notion of abstract equality into the principles of distribution appropriate to each of socialism and communism.

Many of the commentators could agree with this summary. They differ about how to define key terms and about where, of equality, cooperativism, individual liberty, and working-class emancipation, Marx wished to place primary emphasis. They also disagree at a more abstract level about whether or in what ways Marx accepted or rejected supposed theories of ethics or justice. At a similarly abstract level of analysis, one might distinguish two political-philosophical perspectives in accord with which the subjects Marx addresses can be approached. For want of better terms, I shall call these "grand" and "modest" perspectives. Grand political inquiry strives to organize thought about all the potentially related elements of a field of study by comprehending them into a single theory and by postulating necessary relations among them. Modest inquiry seeks contingent relations employing theories appropriate to limited subject matters.[9]

An interpretation of Marx's *Critique* as a modest endeavour would, stressing the work's historicistic dimension, insist that its positive thrust was no more than to prescribe characterizing the first phase of communism as working-class political power, and that other comments function as polemic rhetoric against the normative orientation of the Lassalleans. Alternatively, and in keeping with subsequent appeal to the document to discredit egalitarian socialists, the work lends itself to a more grand theoretical reading. The point can be made by pursuing some distinctions drawn by François Hincker in the lead article of a useful collection of papers published by *Actuel Marx* addressing the question "Has the idea of socialism a future?"[10]

Observing confusing diversity in use of the term "socialism," Hincker distinguishes three broad orders of meaning: as "an intellectual and moral contestation," as a "project for a social alternative," and as a "social and political movement." Abstracting from Hincker's own speculations — he sees socialism, respectively, as anti-individualistic holism, as a thoroughly cooperative society, and as political movements, working-class and otherwise, to secure such a society[11] — the distinction may be employed to explicate a modest approach to theorizing about socialism. On such an approach there is nothing about a characterization of socialism in any one of these contexts that necessitates some one stand regarding the others.

To be sure, answers to the question "What is socialism?" in each context involve both normative-speculative and empirical-descriptive dimensions. To address the largely normative question of socialism as a matter of moral and intellectual contestation, or what I shall call the "socialist ideal," one must pay heed to conceptions in popular political culture if the resulting account is not to become entirely stipulative, while the more empirical effort to identify socialist movements must include some normative judgments to exclude such self-named entities as the National Socialists from counting. Similar considerations pertain to depictions of socialist alternatives. Hence, there will be a certain mutual shaping of inquiries in each domain. Still, the advocate of modest political theory maintains, a variety of packages of responses is possible; or, one might simply remain partially agnostic: It is unnecessary to have a position on everything to advance fruitful thought about some things.

Somebody who, like Hincker, pictures the socialist ideal holistically might disagree with him about socialist movements, thinking that, given the history of association both of Social Democrats and Communists with explicitly class-based politics, the radical wings of working-class movements should have pride of place. Some advocates of market socialism argue for the compatibility of market mechanisms with a cooperativist ethic.[12] Stephen

Cullenberg defends a concept of socialism as "collective appropriation" by reference to "moral primitives," chief among which are egalitarian ideals. (Cullenberg describes collective appropriation as a "thin" concept of socialism, thus illustrating how what are here called socialist alternatives might, like socialist ideals, be modestly or grandly regarded; and the same consideration applies to socialist movements.)[13] Or again, one who pictures socialism as the realization of democracy might nonetheless agree either with Hincker or with Cullenberg about a socialist alternative and defend any of several views on socialist movements, or such a one might remain mute about these things.[14]

Taken as a grand theory, Marx's Gotha *Critique* strives for comprehensiveness and strong connections. The thinking of someone arriving at such a theory might be reconstructed thus:

> The principle agent of socialist transformation is the consciously revolutionary component of the organized working class, due in part to its strength of numbers and its skills of united, cooperative action. Given that the socialist ideal should reflect these strengths but that the socialist alternative must be realistic, a distinction between higher and lower phases allows socialist cooperativism to be more and less strongly interpreted and implemented by the two principles of distribution.

A similar package can be reconstructed hypothesizing a concept of the socialist alternative as a starting place:

> Conceiving of socialism in terms of noncapitalist relations of production, it must be thought of in class terms, as must the transition to it. Given that capitalist relations of production are characterized by competition, all postcapitalist societies must, by contrast, be characterized by cooperation. As progress in socialist production makes the division of labour and hence class divisions superfluous, the similarly more cooperativist distribution of communism will replace that of socialism.

Or the motivating point of orientation might be a concept of the socialist ideal as a perfectly cooperativist society, where

> "[T]he free development of each is the condition for the free development of all."[15] The way will be paved for such a society by a transitional system based on cooperative production, brought into being by the class whose mode of life and work is, as capitalism dialectically digs its own grave, already cooperative.

On the first reconstruction (starting with socialist movements), the progression of thought is motivated by principles governing a class-partisan, power-political way of thinking. The second reconstruction is motivated by a base/superstructure model of economic determinism; while a more philosophically teleological conception of the working class as the bearer of truly human values, such as that examined in Essay 2, could motivate a progression beginning with a projected communist ideal. Whether or not Marx himself is properly interpreted as thinking in terms of one of these models, some such overarching theory is required for a grand approach to the topic of socialism and equality.[16] In particular, such a theory is required to bridge what I take to be the most tenuous association of Marx's *Critique*, namely, that between equality and democratic control of production. Disparaging the Lassallean's call for "democratic control of the 'toiling people,'" Marx properly asks, "but what does 'control by the rule of the people' mean?"[17] The question is apt, and can be addressed to Marx himself respecting his alternative call for "cooperative production on a social scale."[18]

This conception is a fusion of economic, political, and moral elements: pursuit of production in accord with a plan, democratically undertaken, with the purpose of serving, initially, the interests of all who work and, finally, of everyone. Apologists for the late socialism often conflated these elements by conceiving of "proletarian democracy" as equality-guided planning, but it should be evident that the three dimensions of cooperative production are distinct and that democratic control of production must be the core of the notion. In what other way could a collectivity of people, whether all those who work or everyone in society (earlier and later phases of communism in Marx's terms), be said cooperatively to produce on a society-wide scale than by democratically deciding what is to be produced and how?

This, however, leaves open the question of how democratic control of production relates to planning and to equality (either in accord with work or in accord with need). In the *Critique* Marx alleges, consonant with an economic-deterministic mode of thought, that "with the abolition of class distinctions all social and political inequality arising from them would disappear of itself,"[19] but unless interpreted to be trivially true and even allowing that all inequalities are results of class divisions, this is multiply problematic. Presumably, elimination of class divisions makes possible democracy (political equality), including with respect to economic matters, and among the things the citizen-producers decide to do is to eliminate other inequalities.

But there is more than one way that matters of production could be said to be democratically decided. Local, participatory democracy favours some version of workers' self-management somehow combined with effective consumer input. Large-scale representative democratic structures are more compatible with centralized planning, and one can imagine a variety of ways to combine these things. Secondly, while a democratically empowered populace might opt for egalitarian economic and social policies, there is no guarantee that they will, as recent electoral politics in the former socialist countries illustrates. Of course, one may say that the people of these countries are not acting in their true interests, but to deny on this ground that they are acting democratically would be to adopt the self-contradictory model of democracy that was arguably instrumental to the collapse of the authoritarian socialist states. Similarly, there is room for more than one interpretation of what socialist equality might be; candidates include: material equality, equality of opportunity, and political equality.[20]

Both to avoid conceptually confusing conflations and, more importantly, to block the apologies for antidemocratic political practices such confusions facilitate, this paper prescribes a modest approach to thinking about socialism and equality. Such an approach should, in my view, begin by addressing the question of the ideal of socialism, in spite of the fact that this is the most theoretically open of the three dimensions here appropriated from Hincker. Or rather, it should be the starting place precisely because it is the most open domain for theoretical speculation. For socialism to be "unbound," as Stephen Bronner puts it, it must not be identified with "any fixed form of political organization or institutional arrangement."[21] To determine what constitutes a socialist movement or alternative society and then to address the question of a socialist ideal invites forcing thought about the latter into comprehensive frameworks. By contrast, relatively unconstrained thought about a socialist ideal may be grand or modest according to the theorist's predilections.

My own inclination, as summarized in Essay 3, is to portray the ideal of socialism by reference to equality and to do so modestly. The enterprise is modest in two respects. First, to view equality as the ideal of socialism is not therefore to embrace an "egalitarist" position, to employ Texier's term,[22] which holds equality up as the *summum bonum* or as the basis for an entire ethics. Rather, while I remain agnostic on whether there is or must be a highest good or whether moral percepts must have deep ethical foundations, it seems to me that within the context of the contemporary world and with reference to macropolitical values, certain measures and kinds of equality are to be valued instrumentally as preconditions for people gaining control over shared environments. Thus, in a continuum of means and ends, I recommend placing equality in a subordinate position with respect to freedom and, where freedom involves (as in macropolitical situations it always does) collective action, to democracy. The argument for equality in this connection is that persisting inequalities prevent large numbers of people from effectively participating with others in an effort to make shared environments conform to their wishes, even when there are electoral and other formal mechanisms in place ostensibly for this purpose.

Instead of elaborating this argument, often defended by egalitarian socialist theorists,[23] let me now turn to "equality." Here, too, a modest approach can be taken both with reference to the scope of the term and to its interpretation. In the *Critique*, Marx foreshadows many present-day socialists, as in the earlier-cited reference to "social and political equality." By contrast, and in keeping with the notion of socialism as a means, it is here prescribed that the scope of socialist equality be limited to material matters; ignoring nuances, this means to the sorts of things to which monetary value is nonpejoratively and directly assigned. Thus, health care would count, but friendship or political participation would not, even though these latter can be "bought."

Socialists often object to such a limitation, since they think it makes of socialism a crudely materialistic affair. Glowing descriptions of socialism by officials of its late incarnation, it should be noted, did not prevent what called itself "real existing socialism" from being crudely materialistic, and even failing to deliver on its material promises. If the egalitarian socialists' arguments are sound, then relative material equality should provide a basis, if not a guarantee, for other forms of equality; and as the sad experience of authoritarian socialism has shown, a socialist alternative should surely embody political equality and promote social and cultural equality as well. However, unlike grand conceptions of socialism, on the modest approach it is not necessary to build every valued thing that socialism makes possible and each component of a projected socialist alternative into the socialist ideal.

Regarding interpretations of the meaning of "equality," a modest approach abstains from the common practice of seeking a single definition of the term purportedly adequate for policy-making purposes in any circumstances. The debates are well known: Should equality of resources or of results be sought? Is equality to be understood subjectively, or should objective standards be employed? Ought characterization of an egalitarian state of affairs be value neutral, or should it be limited to equality of morally permissible or required state of affairs? And, of course, each option itself involves additional theoretical choices.[24]

To this extent the approach to distribution in the *Critique of the Gotha Programme* was modest: A principle of distribution appropriate to the first phase of communism would not be appropriate to its higher stage. The actual principles Marx endorses are, to be sure, problematic. In addition to the obvious difficulties of ascertaining in lower communism whether and to what extent a "contribution" has been made and how to determine the level of subsidization of those who cannot work (a large majority if one considers the very aged, the ill, and children), there is a problem identifying what counts as work. The higher phase of communism is distinguished from the first phase by Marx in part by the fact that in full communism, work has become "life's prime want."[25]

Whether through neurosis or good fortune, however, this will also be true for some in communism's first phase, as it now is for those privileged few in capitalist society who hold intrinsically rewarding jobs. At the same time, it is hard to imagine even a classless society where absolutely all work will be thus rewarding. Is, then, an effort to be made to balance benefits and burdens in both phases of communism? If so, the sharp distributive distinction Marx wants to draw is blurred. Nonetheless, the strategy of making types of prescribed equality context sensitive can be followed by a modest egalitarian theorist.

Theorizing about equality in this mode is facilitated by avoiding egalitarism. If equality is not thought of as the pivot of an ethical theory, there is no onus to produce a concept applicable to all circumstances. This abstinence also suggests a solution to the problem of whether equality should be normatively characterized.[26] If equality is seen as one element in means-end continua, then one can *presumptively* prescribe egalitarian social policy, where what is to be equalized is nonnormatively described, with the understanding that such prescriptions are overridable in those situations where egalitarian distribution would not serve its supposed ends.

Modest egalitarian theorizing is also facilitated by confining itself, as Marx did with respect to the first phase of communism but not to the higher stage, to existing circumstances and to imaginary future ones, which are such that realistic paths from present realities to their realization can be described. Though it goes beyond the topic of this paper, one should note that this limitation encourages socialist politics that, in the manner favoured by Gramsci or Macpherson, builds as much as possible on presocialist political institutions and cultures.

A treatment by the egalitarian socialist G. A. Cohen is appropriate here by way of illustration. In an often-cited article, "Robert Nozick and Wilt Chamberlain: How Patterns Preserve Liberty," he challenges Nozick's charge that socialism would be unjustifiably freedom constraining. Nozick imagines a situation in an egalitarian society where sports fans want to reward a talented athlete, such as the now-retired basketball player Wilt Chamberlain, but would be prohibited from doing so to maintain equality of income. This is then supposed to be a paradigm of how equality objection-ably constrains freedom. Cohen maintains that this argument requires one to project values held in capitalist society into a future socialism where, con-trary to Nozick's assumption, people will not *want* to create power imbal-ances because, highly valuing egalitarian socialism, they will not wish to allow anyone to gain means to disproportionate power.[27]

A generic merit of Cohen's view is that it allows him to conceive of socialist equality in subjective and nonnormative terms (thus avoiding democracy-threatening attempts to dictate needs or legislate preferences) while escaping the problem faced by preference-satisfaction egalitarians of accommodating equality-disrupting and otherwise objectionable preferences. Its disadvan-tage is that it depends upon unproven assumptions about what preferences people in a future society will have. On the modest egalitarian approach, Cohen's implied characterization of advanced socialist equality is acceptable if one can construct and defend a theory explicating mechanisms by which the value transformations he refers to might actually come about. Inability to adduce plausible mechanisms would not mean that Cohen has failed to produce a viable ideal for a distant socialist society (which is all he needed to counter the explicit utopian, Nozick), but it would tell against employing the implied concept to articulate a socialist ideal for the contemporary world.

Perhaps the most contentious point of debate among theorists concerning themselves with material equality is over whether what is to be equalized is, as far as possible, satisfaction of people's existing preferences (a subjective interpretation of well-being) or something objective, such as provision for basic needs or, as in Macpherson's view and more recently defended by many egalitarians trying to retrieve some Aristotle-like theory of proper human functions,[28] that which is required for people to develop their truly human potentials. A decision in either direction brings problems in its wake, though different problems.

The subjectivist must confront such facts as that preferences are idiosyn-cratic and sometimes bizarre, that they can be deliberately manipulated and indirectly shaped by accommodating to available resources, that interper-sonal comparisons are often hard to make, and that preference conflicts among people are common. Objectivists escape these sorts of problems, but they require a theory to specify that which is sufficiently important to humans that social policies should strive to equalize it. Not only does this drive the egalitarian objectivist into deep philosophical water, but the result-ing prescriptions would override preferences, thus promoting paternalism.

It is therefore not surprising that each of objectivist and subjectivist egalitarians tries to temper his or her approach. An example of a position close to the middle may be found in a more recent treatment by Cohen. He urges that what should be equalized are opportunities and capacities to enjoy "advantages," provided that deficiencies in these respects do not result from one's own noncoerced choices.[29] This conception is deliberately vague about whether "advantage" should be subjectively or objectively interpreted, and situations come to mind when it is problematic whether people's choices are coerced. However, some such conception seems to me a suitable base from which to construct a generic socialist ideal. My own inclination is to purchase the problems of a preference-satisfaction conception of "advantage" primarily in order to avoid paternalistic dangers I see in a competing objective notion. This does not mean, however, that identification of appropriate opportunities and capacities is also subjective.

Also, while something like Cohen's approach may suffice as a general egalitarian conception suitable to socialist employment, the term "advantage" (taken to include an irreducible subjective component) needs to be interpreted. Here, the historically contextualized orientation of the *Critique* referred to above may be instructive. Put in egalitarian terms, the advantages to be distributed in the first and second phases of communism are, respectively, gainful employment and satisfaction of needs. It is not clear whether Marx himself would have sanctioned partially subjective interpretations of these things: that people are not to be forced to do work hateful to them, for instance, and that preferences are to be taken into account in ascertaining needs.

An egalitarian employing either of these two possible objects of equalization will confront the difficulties purchased on any subjective interpretation, but, at least in the case of "desired work," policy guidelines are suggested that make the task less daunting in the concrete than in the abstract. People's recalcitrance to do certain sorts of work invites the egalitarian to seek realistic measures to bring distribution of jobs into phase with people's preferences: provision of job alternatives; technological innovation; reorganization of workplaces; special incentives; and so on. Marx's contextualizations are historical, thus allowing one to wait for the anticipated, dramatically changed, if only vaguely specified, conditions of life and work before confronting problems such as how to meet all of everybody's needs. The demise of confidence in historical metaphysics means that contemporary socialists no longer have such luxury.

Rather than sorting advantages that socialist distribution of material opportunities and capacities is supposed to secure by reference to historical phases, I choose to sort them into those that are *proactive* (having to do with realizing desired goals) and *reactive* (escaping undesired constraints). Perhaps securing gainful and desired employment should be endorsed by socialists as a main proactive advantage. However, it seems to me that one might aim rather higher. In Essay 8 it will be argued that socialism's unique contribution to an environmentally sustainable globe could be the provision of capabilities and opportunities for people to pursue a meaningful life as they see it. Those for whom this means doing talent-employing labour (for whom work is "life's prime want") should thus be (presumptively) accommodated, while recognizing that not all will see a meaningful life this way. Perhaps, as in the case of work, questions of distribution will be less problematic when actually confronted than in high egalitarian theory. In Essay 8 further comments will be made about the subjective nature of this conception.

In the remainder of this essay I shall articulate my choice for a socialist ideal regarded reactively, drawing initially on Iris Marion Young's conception of justice. For her, a theory of justice in today's world should be explicitly linked to the problem of overcoming oppression and domination: sexist, classist, racist, and so on.[30] Recognizing the complexities involved in defining such terms, and despite their often merely rhetorical use in radical politics, I shall refer to this as a counteroppressive concept of justice. "Oppression" is regarded as the morally objectionable, systematic thwarting of the aspirations of nearly everyone in some category, where part of what makes this systematic is that their aspirations are impeded in an ongoing and predictable way even when this cannot be explained by reference to ill will or malicious intention on the part of others.[31]

The subjective element in this definition allows that when a sufficient number of people in a category are "happy in their servitude," we only have a case of potential oppression. This allowance poses some problems for democratic theorists,[32] but for socialist egalitarians there are all too many examples of undeniable oppression to occupy them. Systemic discrimination against women or members of racial minorities are two examples, as is the downward spiral peoples of the underdeveloped world find themselves in. As the work of Young and many other radical scholars has shown, the originating and sustaining causes of oppression, thus defined, are many and varied, as are the ways to try to overcome them. However, among the sustaining causes of all major oppressive situations today are material inequalities. These simultaneously deny those who suffer oppression the means to acquire the capacities and opportunities to overcome them, and afford those who profit from the domination of others the means to maintain their advantages.

Young's treatment is not idiosyncratic to her, but represents variations on themes currently addressed by scholars who place themselves on the political left. They take as their points of departure one or more of the several forms of systemic discrimination and other forms of structural oppression evident to everyone except the ideologically blinded as pervasive features of all existing societies. Regarded as a (reactive) ideal, then, socialism may be characterized as the achievement of those measures and kinds of material equality required to provide people with the capacities and opportunities to overcome structural oppressions. The ideal is modest in being valued as just one moment in counteroppressive politics rather than as an end in itself, in being confined to material equality; and in being advanced as a necessary but not a sufficient precondition for overcoming domination or oppression.[33] Conceived in this way, the notion may also be more or less widely applied depending on whether it is relativized to specific oppressions.

For instance, a "socialist-feminist" on this view is one concerned to overcome sexist oppression and who advocates those measures and kinds of material equality required to this end. Such a person may *also* advocate equality necessary for overcoming any other forms of oppression sustained by material inequality, as might a socialist concerned to end working-class oppression, racism, or national oppression, to name main examples. Given the ways such oppressions mutually reinforce one another,[34] the differences in practice between programmes required effectively to act on the socialist ideal fully and more narrowly advanced are likely smaller than the large diversity of motivations for favouring socialist equality might suggest. Cohen's focus on opportunities and capacities fits the counteroppressive dimension of this characterization, since systemic discrimination and other forms of oppression typically function in large measure by denying these things, and antioppressive movements accordingly place the demand for substantive equal opportunity, including access to means for developing potentials, at the centres of their campaigns.

Classifying counteroppressive equality as "reactive" does not mean that socialist politics guided by it can or should be carried on only by those in oppressed groups, and by those who see themselves and are seen as nothing but "interest groups." In addition to considerations about how accurate such a picture of social movements is (the point will be pursued in Essay 7), it is doubtful that behaviour consonant with the socialist ideal could be motivated entirely by considerations of self-interest. Some concern for the well-being of others likely needs to be part of the popular culture of any society in which the socialist ideal is to be more than a rallying cry of minority dissidents. Should proposals about just what value transformations are needed to this end and how to achieve them be incorporated into a socialist ideal?

Perhaps it ought to be made explicit that an egalitarian society is one in which people are at least partly motivated by concern for the well-being of others. This would capture the moral element of the notion that a socialist society is "cooperative." However, in keeping with the modest approach here recommended, other considerations about the preconditions for socialism and the means for realizing it are best addressed in the context of socialist alternatives and socialist movements. Thus, hypotheses about the coordination of production to serve both local and global egalitarian ends (the economic and political elements of cooperativism) are best addressed in the construction of proposed socialist alternatives. Such proposals, like those about what benefits and burdens are to be equally distributed, no doubt should be explicated in models for alternatives sensitive to a society's specific circumstances. Prosocialist, movement politics should, again in ways specific to a movement and its local circumstances, be explicitly carried on in such a way as to facilitate appropriate changes of values.

This brings us back to these two dimensions of socialism, about which I will only make some observations flowing from the above proposal for a socialist ideal. In general, a socialist alternative is any projected social/political/economic arrangement, one intended aim of which is to realize counteroppressive, material equality. It is unlikely that any one sort or combination of structures (e.g., central planning, constrained markets, parliamentary and/or extraparliamentary political forms) could be devised suitable to advancing material equality in all societies. Given the diversity of the world's societies and the interdependence among states, substate locales, and superstate regions, there is no doubt that devising egalitarian institutions is extraordinarily challenging; however, this is all the more reason not to try to build institutional designs into the ideal of socialism.

As to "socialist movements," it should be noted that this term ambiguously describes both movements that have it as their aim to promote socialism and movements that promote socialism in the course of advancing other goals. A main topic of debate among movement activists is whether or how anything other than minimum coordination of the latter type of movements is required. Though it goes beyond the intent of this paper to pursue the topic, I rather think that something more is needed; and in any case political parties or wings of parties already exist in most countries that include as central parts of a platform the promotion of material equality. On the conception of socialism suggested above, such parties or wings, whatever their members call them, are properly designated "socialist" when the measure and kinds of equality they promote would in fact have significant counteroppressive potential.

Let me conclude with a few comments in the direction of immodesty. Not a few whom I consider socialist egalitarians demur at the use of the word "equality" and/or the word "socialism." It is not uncommon to find socialists who prefer calling for the elimination of inequalities rather than the promotion of equality,[35] among other reasons, because the latter term carries connotations of plannification and, as Marx's comments in the Gotha *Critique* indicate, of levelling. To respond by shifting attention from equality to anti-inequality seems, however, excessively defensive. It has largely been *anti*egalitarians who have tried to identify equality with simplistic equal treatment,[36] and egalitarians should challenge such identification rather than capitulate to it.

If "plannification" refers to the sort of hierarchical, closed economic systems that have just failed, then, again, the egalitarian need not be identified with it. However, thought of as planning, the situation is different. To a certain extent, egalitarian policies *will* require planning, in part to compensate for unequal distribution of a society's benefits and burdens by providing appropriate equal distribution. To pretend otherwise is either to misrepresent egalitarianism (or anti-inegalitarianism) or to denude it of effectiveness. Egalitarians would be better advised to grant, indeed to insist, that appropriate economic planning is indispensable to promoting equality and to turn their attention to ways this can be done flexibly and democratically.

A similar point pertains to "socialism." No amount of rhetoric can disguise the radical nature of politics that embraces the ideal of counteroppressive material equality. The appropriate contrast is capitalism, where this is interpreted as a system institutionally structured around the presumption that the main means of production and distribution are privately owned, such that those who own them may do what they wish with profits.[37] An empirical claim of all socialists is that, "trickle-down" theorists to the contrary, such a system cannot provide enough in the way of material equality to make possible the overcoming of what in this essay are called structural oppressions. It is understandable that in the post-1989 world, some radical egalitarians would see a political advantage to dropping the term "socialism." A contrary recommendation is suggested by situating the *Critique of the Gotha Programme* within a certain viewpoint on modernity.

One of Marx's criticisms of the Lassalleans was that they failed to recognize the abstract nature of bourgeois concepts of equal rights, which, he maintained, masked the fact that in capitalist society, workers are conceived of *"only as workers*, and nothing more is seen in them, everything else is ignored."[38] Texier concludes that Marx was anticipating a contrasting communist society that "transcends equality," where individuals are able to develop in all their aspects.[39] Nielsen recognizes that something like this picture is the ideal of the communist principle "From each according to ability, to each according to need," but observes that in anything less than a situation of impossibly complete abundance, burdens and benefits will still have to be shared. He maintains that the communist principle governing distribution in any such situation is not beyond equality, but is in the spirit of "our primitive sense of justice" whereby "we must start from an equal consideration of the interests of everyone."[40]

I have suggested how, on a modest conception of socialism, the perspectives of Texier and Nielsen can be reconciled: Socialist material equality is valued as a means for facilitating postoppressive freedom. However, now it is appropriate to ask whether, in accord with Nielsen's perspective, socialist/communist principles represent the full realization of abstract equal rights or, as in Texier's account, they are an alternative to them. According to one viewpoint on modernity, best articulated in a way that relates to this discussion by Jacques Bidet,[41] neither alternative is exactly accurate. On this perspective, a presumption in favour of (abstractly considered) equal respect for all individuals is part of a uniquely modern system of values, associated with such other notions as that state authority gains legitimacy from contracts among freely choosing individuals. That from very early in the modern era actual choices have been far from free and few people have enjoyed respectful treatment, due in part to economic constraints perpetuated by capitalism, does not mean that as an ideal abstract equality is a specifically bourgeois notion.

Depending on one's favoured philosophical approach, such equality might be viewed as a floating signifier, as an abstract universal, or simply as a concept admitting of various interpretations. In any case, the modern ideal of equality on this perspective is to be viewed as a field of contest (rather than as the necessary property of one contestant) on which two of the major competing interpretations historically have been procapitalist and prosocialist. For advocates of the former, deviations from exclusively juridic equality must be specially justified; for the socialists—however they have located equality with respect to other ends—a presumption of something in the way of substantive, material equality has been defended. The ideal of equality is, as Hincker notes about the ideal of socialism, one of contestation.

This means that socialism cannot simply be identified with egalitarianism, since it is the interpretation of this latter ideal that is at issue. Nor, it seems to me, should the term be replaced by "deep egalitarianism" or the like, and this for two reasons. First, in the contests over equality in modern political culture, socialism is already associated with the radical alternative. In any case, to reject the term as if there were something to be ashamed of about its use would make it all the more attractive for those advancing the narrower, capitalist-serving alternative to remind people of the historic association.

Secondly, notwithstanding—or perhaps partly because of—Marx's ambiguous efforts in the *Critique of the Gotha Programme*, that stream of socialist theory and practice oriented around vanguard, working-class-dictatorship politics did not dissociate itself from the ideal of socialist equality. Rather, it came to be associated with the pursuit of equality, albeit not clearly interpreted, and with the resulting bad name socialist equality has acquired. Should the recent, nearly worldwide triumph of a capitalist ideal wane, as capitalism fails to live up to its promises (predictably in my view), it would be most unfortunate if, again given the association of socialism with anticapitalism in popular consciousness, it were thought that the now discredited version of socialism is its only alternative.

Notes

1. Karl Marx, *Critique of the Gotha Programme*, in Lewis Feuer, ed., *Marx & Engels Basic Writings on Politics and Philosophy* (Garden City, NY: Doubleday Anchor, 1959), chap. 5, 119–20.
2. Etienne Balibar, *Sur la dictature du prolétariat* (Paris: Librairie François Maspero, 1976), see 268–75.
3. For example, in his "'Droits de l'homme' et 'droits du citoyen': La dialectique modern de l'égalité et de la liberté," *Actuel Marx*, No. 8 (Deuxième semestre, 1990), 13–32.
4. Kai Nielsen, "Marx, Engels and Lenin on Justice: *The Critique of the Gotha Programme*," in a collection of his papers on this subject, *Marxism and the Moral Point of View* (Boulder, CO: Westview Press, 1989), chap. 4, 70.
5. Jacques Texier, "Marx, penseur égalitaire?," *Actuel Marx*, No. 8 (Deuxième semestre, 1990), 45–66.
6. I have criticized the power-political orientation in my *Democratic Theory and Socialism* (Cambridge: Cambridge University Press, 1987), 150–67. References to the debates about Marx and justice may be found in the above-cited article of Nielsen and in a survey by Stefano Petrucciani, "Marx et la critique de l'égalité politique," *Actuel Marx*, No. 8 (Duexième semestre, 1990), 67–86. A treatment claiming that Marx defended equal liberty (thus combining the orientations of Marx and Texier) and including many references to the debate about Marx and justice is R. G. Peffer, *Marxism, Morality, and Social Justice* (Princeton, NJ: Princeton University Press, 1990).
7. Marx, *Critique*, 119.
8. *Ibid.*, 127.
9. What is here called modest theorizing I defend as "philosophy of the middle range" in my *Democratic Theory* (see chap. 2). The distinction "grand/modest" is

compatible with, but not identical to, that between "foundationism" and "anti-foundationism."

10. François Hincker, *L'idée du socialisme: A-t-elle un avenir?* publication of Actuel Marx Confrontation (Paris: Presses Universitaires de France, 1992).

11. François Hincker, "Du passé (socialiste) faut-il faire table rase?" *ibid.*, 13–18. Hincker's use of "socialist alternative" usually makes the term synonymous with "intellectual and moral contestation" (thus allowing him confusingly to advance more than one version of what is here called "the socialist ideal"). I shall reserve the term "socialist alternative" for prescriptions about political and economic arrangements thought to further whatever is taken to be the ideal of socialism. It is interesting that Eric Hobsbawm, also a socialist historian, in a publication analogous to that of *Actuel Marx*, advances the same hypothesis about what Hincker calls socialism as moral contestation, except Hobsbawm adds that the object of socialist collectivism is "at bottom a demand for social justice," "Out of the Ashes," in Robin Blackburn, ed., *After the Fall: The Failure of Communism and the Future of Socialism* (London: Verso, 1991), 315–25, 316.

12. For instance, Joseph Carens, *Equality, Moral Incentives and the Market* (Chicago: University of Chicago Press, 1981).

13. Stephen Cullenberg, "Socialism's Burden: Toward a 'Thin' Definition of Socialism," *Rethinking Marxism*, Vol. 5, No. 2 (Summer 1992), 64–83, see 80. In this same issue of *Rethinking Marxism*, the contributions of David Ruccio ("Failure of Socialism, Future of Socialists?") and of Ronald Aronson ("After Communism") advance yet additional, similarly modest conceptions of dimensions of socialism.

14. In my book *Democratic Theory and Socialism*, I defend an egalitarian view of socialism, remaining more or less agnostic about the nature of a socialist alternative and movements for socialism. It now seems to me that the egalitarian ideal was insufficiently theorized in the book.

15. Karl Marx and Frederick Engels, *Manifesto of the Communist Party*, in Lewis Feuer, ed., *Marx & Engels Basic Writings on Politics and Philosophy* (Garden City, NY: Doubleday Anchor, 1959), chap. 3, 29.

16. As I read Marx there is a tension in his thought between modest and grand theoretical tendencies. As a modest theorist he was primarily concerned to demonstrate that the economic and moral weaknesses of capitalism were not accidents. To theorize in a modest fashion is not to reject theory. An example of an attempt to construct a perspective both modest and sufficiently strong to serve the end of combatting oppressions is the "materialist pragmatism" elaborated in *Democratic Theory*, chap. 9.

17. Marx, *Critique*, 125–26.

18. *Ibid.*, 126.

19. *Ibid.*, 125.

20. Thus, like Nielsen, I attempt to elaborate a concept of socialism in terms of material equality. Andrew Levine defends socialism as the realization of equality of opportunity, *Arguing for Socialism* (Boston: Routledge & Kegan Paul, 1984) (although in his other books he contrasts this concept with cooperativism). For Carol Gould, socialism is primarily regarded as political equality, "Socialism and Democracy," *Praxis International*, Vol. 1, No. 1 (April 1981), 49–63.

21. Stephen Eric Bronner, *Socialism Unbound* (New York: Routledge, 1990), 147.

22. Thus Texier criticizes the "égalitristes" for upholding the "value of equality to

the exclusion of all other values" ("Marx," 64). And Nielsen avoids the construction of fundamental ethical theory to defend his prescriptions. See chap. 1 of *Marxism and the Moral Point of View*.

23. That equality is a precondition for democratic progress is a central argument of my *Democratic Theory*. See, too, Philip Green, *Retrieving Democracy* (Totowa, NJ: Rowman & Allanheld, 1985); Andrew Levine, *Arguing for Socialism*; and Kai Nielsen, *Equality and Liberty: A Defense of Radical Egalitarianism* (Totowa, NJ: Rowman & Allanheld, 1985).

24. A useful summary of recent debates over defining "equality" is found in an article by G. A. Cohen, "On the Currency of Egalitarian Justice," *Ethics*, Vol. 99, No. 4 (July 1989), 906–44. See, too, Louise Marcil-Lacoste, *La thématique contemporaine de l'égalité: Répetoire, résumés, typologie* (Montréal: Les Presses de l'Université de Montréal, 1984).

25. Marx, *Critique*, 119.

26. A summary of the debate and a defence of "perfectionism" by Thomas Hurka may be found in Rodger Beehler *et al.*, eds., *On the Track of Reason: Essays in Honor of Kai Nielsen* (Boulder, CO: Westview Press, 1992), chap. 2.

27. G. A. Cohen, "Robert Nozick and Wilt Chamberlain: How Patterns Preserve Liberty," in John Arthur and William H. Shaw, eds., *Justice and Economic Distribution* (Englewood Cliffs, NJ: Prentice-Hall, 1978), 246–62.

28. The most prominent of these theorists, and one who applies egalitarian theory to third world situations and other real-life problems, is Amartya Sen. See his recent book, *Inequality Reexamined* (Cambridge, MA: Harvard University Press, 1992).

29. G. A. Cohen, "Currency."

30. Iris Marion Young, *Justice and the Politics of Difference* (Princeton, NJ: Princeton University Press, 1990), see chaps. 1 and 2.

31. For definitions of "oppression" see Iris Marion Young, *Justice and the Politics of Difference*, chap. 2; Thomas Wartenberg, *The Forms of Power: From Domination to Transformation* (Philadelphia: Temple University Press, 1990), 117; and my *Democratic Theory*, 203–4.

32. The generic problem is that of "false consciousness," discussed in Essay 1, and treated at length in *Democratic Theory and Socialism*, chap. 10. In my view, the problem for egalitarians posed by the example of the "happy slave" makes it all the more important to integrate the egalitarian and the democratic projects. One virtue of a highly democratic society is that people are able to interact with one another in such a way as to question the wisdom, or otherwise, of their own and others' values.

33. Contrasting this prescribed conception with the similarly motivated one of Jacques Texier may help to explicate it. Texier maintains that for any project to count as socialist it must aim at "the abolition of privileges of all sorts: those of power, of culture and of wealth," and he adds that "because the world system is dominated by the power of capital . . . these structural reforms are 'socialist,' when they attack the power of capital." "Quelle culture pour quel concept de la politique?" *L'idée du socialisme*, 255–80, at 276 (translation by F.C.). The notion of counteroppressive material equality is compatible with the first part of Texier's description, provided it is clearly understood that combatting privilege is a necessary but not also a sufficient condition for something to be a socialist project. Socialism is more narrowly conceived than Texier's account if he wishes

to build success in overcoming all forms of privilege definitionally into "socialism." Also, the feature of capitalism that socialism aims to overcome (certain material inequalities) is specified. Texier would unquestionably agree that socialism must attack other sources of inequality, such as bureaucratic privilege, as well.

34. The mutual reinforcement of oppressions is well explicated by feminist socialists. For some examples, among many, see the contributions to Zillah Eisenstein, ed., *Capitalist Patriarchy and the Case for Socialist Feminism* (New York: Monthly Review Press, 1979).

35. This is the point of view, for example, of Veit Bader and Albert Benschop, *Ungleichheiten* (Opladen, Germany: Leske, 1989).

36. See Young, *Difference*, chap. 6. An explication of the logic and the effects of the identification of identity and equality may be found in Louise Marcil-Lacoste's *La Raison en procès* (Ville de LaSalle, P.Q.: Brèches, 1987), see chaps. 6–8 and concluding section.

37. I explicate this more or less Marxist conception of capitalism in *Democratic Theory*, chap. 5.

38. Marx, *Critique*, ·1420.

39. Texier, "Marx," 61, and see 54–58.

40. Nielsen, "Marx," 92.

41. Jacques Bidet, *Marx et le marché* (Paris: Presses Universitaires de France, 1990). An extract of the book bearing on the application of this perspective to Marx and equality is "Liberté, égalité, modernité," *Actuel Marx*, No. 8 (Deuxième semestre, 1990), 87–102. See, too, Bidet's *Théorie de la modernité* (Paris: Presses Universitaires de France, 1990), see especially, I.i, I.4. For a historical application that well illustrates the contestational character of equality, see the book on Hobbes by Mario Reale, *La difficile eguaglianza* (Rome: Editori Riuniti, 1991).

ESSAY 5

Democracy and Socialism: Philosophical Aporiae

"aporia": inter alia,
"embarrassment, perplexity"

There can be little doubt that the history of what in its twilight years called itself "real existing socialism" has proven an embarrassment to *Marxist* philosophy as officially interpreted in this socialism. In form, that philosophy was proposed as a general world view: a vision of the good society and the good life supported by a critique of dominant views about what is possible and desirable, a metaphysics, and prescriptions for how to realize the vision.

The Marxist vision pictured an egalitarian and cooperative society in which unrewarding and narrowly confining labour had been overcome. The critique argued that doctrines such as "people are naturally selfish or un-equal" are system-reinforcing expressions of life in a capitalist society. Dialectical materialism provided an ontology and logic. And historical materialism supported the prescription that the dictatorship of the proletariat, exercised by those who understand working-class objective interests, should transform capitalist society to communism. The authoritarian societies of which this was the state philosophy are the ones now being overturned in Eastern Europe and the Soviet Union.

This essay was published in *Philosophy & Social Criticism*, Vol. 16, No. 4 (1990). Earlier versions were read in the Centre for Theoretical Studies in the Humanities and the Social Sciences, University of Essex, and at the 1990 Eastern Division American Philosophical Association meetings. I have profited from comments at these sessions and from criticisms by Harry Kunneman and Peter Pekelharing.

To be sure, one dimension of Marxist philosophy suggests an avenue for partial disembarrassment by arguing that it, no more than any other system of ideas, could be the cause of such phenomena. However, as discussed in Essay 2, it is hard to deny that aspects of the perspective just outlined were sustaining causes. The proto-paternalistic doctrine of working-class objective interests perpetuated a mystified, antidemocratic concentration of political power in which stifling democratic rights was sanctioned in the name of a higher form of democracy. Marxist metaphysics provided the authoritarian state with an official philosophy by reference to which alternative world views were identified and suppressed. Insofar as the critique and the vision counterposed egalitarian planning to markets, cast aspersion on liberal-democratic protection of individual rights, and pictured all (postclass-society) conflict as pernicious, they were surely implicated in the hypercentralized plannification, wholesale rejection of liberalism, and antipluralism now under attack.

Perhaps there are some Marxist philosophers who wish to defend both the erstwhile real existing socialism and the official-line Marxism associated with it, or some may continue to espouse such Marxism but claim that it was improperly put into practice. On stronger grounds are socialist philosophers who reject some or all of what I have described as the official line (among whom there is a secondary distinction between non-Marxist socialists, who think this line sanctioned by Marxist texts, and Marxists, who think it a distortion).[1] How embarrassing the debacle of real existing socialism is to socialist philosophers depends upon how far removed from official-line Marxism their alternative theories are. Those who applaud the current democratic rejection of authoritarianism while lamenting rejection of equality as a politically realizable goal and who, agreeing with Marx's critique of capitalism, also wish to continue resisting what Macpherson aptly called the "possessive individualist culture" it sustains confront a difficult task.

THE RETRIEVALIST OPTION

One direction is to attempt a marriage between socialist and liberal-democratic theory. Macpherson himself saw this "retrievalist" effort as the most appropriate direction for first world socialists, as in different ways do some social democrats and advocates of market socialism.[2] Emboldened by events in Eastern Europe, many liberal democrats challenge such projects, maintaining that liberal-democratic political philosophy unalloyed with socialist dimensions is not at all problematic in today's world, that it has nothing to be embarrassed about. At the end of this paper, I shall return to the question of whether there is a specifically liberal-democratic philosophy. Let it be noted here that to the extent that liberal-democratic politics can claim philosophical ancestry, it is questionable that its ancestors have no cause for embarrassment.

Political practice in the name of liberal democracy has supported morally indefensible domestic and global inequalities; racism, sexism, and national chauvinism; a culture of alienating individualism, competitiveness, and consumerism; and (despite the highly publicized claims advanced by the Rand Corporation's Francis Fukuyama) war.[3] Of course, the liberal democrat, like the socialist making an analogous claim, can maintain that such practice violates liberal-democratic values. Setting aside the historical dimensions of such defences, this paper examines some recent philosophical (or metaphilosophical) debates pertaining to liberal democracy in a way that I hope will contribute to the project of its socialist retrieval.

Those wishing to combine socialist egalitarianism and liberal democracy typically identify as a main shortcoming of liberal-democratic theory its failure to recognize structural sources of illiberal and antidemocratic practices, which failure is sometimes attributed simply to hypocrisy and sometimes to dispensable aspects of the theory, such as an excessively narrow or formal concept of freedom. Other socialists perceive in liberal democracy a social ontology so alien to cooperativist or egalitarian values as to be irredeemable.[4] While recent, widespread rejection of nonliberal-democratic socialism strengthens the retrievalist socialists' position in their dispute with antiretrievalists, retrievalists purchase more than the problem of showing that socialism and liberal democracy are not oil and water. They must also confront a well-known problem for liberal-democratic theory itself.

A central liberal-democratic value against which the theory and practice of real existing socialism enthusiastically pitted itself is pluralism: the injunction that political society should protect the ability of people to pursue their own goods in their own ways. It is all too obvious how socialism violated pluralism, but it should not go unnoticed that liberal democracy also is in tension with its own core value. As recent debates between liberal democrats and their communitarian critics illustrate, liberal democrats must insist on the preeminence of liberal values over respect for conflicting communally supported ones, even though members of the community are pursuing their own goods as they see them.

Among their responses (the evaluation of which will occupy Essay 6 of this collection) has been the appropriate observation by liberal democrats that not to give the rights associated with liberal neutrality preeminence is to sanction antidemocratic rule by sometimes-oppressive tradition. Unless socialists are to repeat the mistake of rejecting pluralism, they must find a way to incorporate some analogue of liberal-democratic neutrality. Insofar as retrievalist socialists wish to highlight certain values, such as cooperation or equality, they will find this in tension with neutrality, and at the same time they will confront this apparently paradoxical feature of liberal democracy.

Assuming that authoritarian socialism has been an embarrassment to Marxist philosophy and at least poses a perplexing problem for other socialists, this paper takes, as a point of entry to the question of how pluralism poses a problem for each of socialist and liberal-democratic political theory and practice, some observations about how philosophy *per se* is democratically problematic. I do not suggest that this is the only or even the best approach to the nest of *aporiae* here addressed, but it is at least one avenue appropriately explored by professional philosophers, and it can take advantage of some recent stimulating exercises in philosophical self-examination.

Philosophy and Pluralism

Philosophy is here taken to be the attempted union of the articulation and defence of visions of the world,[5] on the one hand, and radical critique, on the other. Full-blown visionary philosophy includes normative and extranormative dimensions and strives to be systematic. Such pursuit is less in vogue today than in other times, having given way to a fragmentation of the discipline. However, I have the impression that it is participation in the manner of a division of labour that gives the subdisciplines of philosophy their claim on this name, provided that each conjoins its chosen task with the dogged critique of its own and others' principles and methods.[6]

Democracy, as I think of it, requires, among other things, institutions and political-cultural habits that facilitate reaching consensus or peacefully negotiating conflicts on the part of people engaged in the effort to make shared environments conform to their various preferences.[7] Since people's preferences differ, among other things, over life aims or visions of the good society, and it is not always possible to reach consensus or even desirable to try, pluralistic mutual tolerance is an important precondition for ongoing democratic practices.

Philosophers sometimes maintain that the study of philosophy contributes to democracy by providing training in critical thought and by making explicit the principles informing the world views found among a society's population, thus promoting mutual understanding. While philosophical study undoubtedly does have these potentials, it seems no less undeniable that there are tensions between philosophy and democracy. Critical thinking can lead to destructive scepticism. The articulation of visions of the world can serve to rationalize the dogmatically entrenched tenets of a society's dominant tradition; or if the visions are novel, "utopian" ones, it can promote contempt for the traditional viewpoints of *hoi polloi.*

These propensities derive in part from the fact that the philosophical enterprise is radical. Those philosophers who defend utopian world views are driven to reject established alternative viewpoints. Like the philosopher as radical critic, the utopians thus invite the hemlock. Those philosophers who, arriving as the Owl of Minerva, set out to defend the world view of an existing tradition must give thoroughgoing reasons of the sort any philosopher worth his or her salt is good at producing to justify the tradition, thus entrenching it yet further.

Regarding these ways that democracy constitutes a problem for philosophy, I would like to address two sorts of approaches that (without wishing much to hinge on the labels) I shall call "historicistic" and "transcendental." Philosophers like Richard Rorty, Michael Walzer, or Alasdair MacIntyre situate philosophy within the community-specific cultural traditions that, they argue, give people who inhabit them a sense of their identities and provide appropriate norms of behaviour. Rorty views traditions as more homogeneous and closed to one another than do the other communitarians, which gives his approach both an advantage and a disadvantage with respect to democracy. The advantage is that he can consistently argue that in a society where traditions include a democratic political culture, philosophy cannot but be democracy serving.[8] This position has the limitation that whether and how philosophy can be coordinated with democracy depends upon the accident of the times and places of its pursuit.

A response from within this "historicist" camp is to adopt a broader concept of democracy than Rorty's, which seems simply to identify it with U.S.-style government, and speak of a democratic role for philosophy from within any tradition insofar as, by encouraging autocritique and by motivating visions, philosophers promote participation in collective decision making within that tradition and toleration toward other traditions. This approach is suggested by MacIntyre's contention that traditions are susceptible of change when they cease to progress in terms of their own criteria or when they encounter alternative traditions to which they could potentially accommodate themselves.[9] One might speculate that it is the unique function of philosophy to alert one to the possibility and desirability of progressive change and accommodation, where "progress" is defined by reference to democracy. Walzer comes close to expressing such a view in his description of the "company of critics": those practice-oriented intellectuals from a wide variety of communities who, despite their tradition-specific differences, share a critical concern with democratic values.[10]

Though I believe there is much of merit in the communitarian theories, they seem in the present context rather to highlight difficulties involved in relating philosophy to democracy than to offer solutions. To the extent that members of the company of critics are radical in their criticisms, they are, as Walzer notes, in danger of becoming isolated from their communities—the hemlock problem. Insofar as a tradition contains no explicitly recognized criterion of democratic progress or counsels hostility toward what is alien, the tradition-bound philosopher can perform antidemocratic functions—the Owl of Minerva problem.

A "transcendental" approach attempts simultaneously to solve both problems by demonstrating that in any human community there must be the germ of a democratic morality, and that a prescription for nurturing this is at the heart of a philosophical theory of ethics. If the demonstration of these things is inescapably rigorous, then this ethical prescription and its political concomitants should be endorsed by all philosophers. One celebrated effort of this sort is that of Jürgen Habermas (which he calls "quasi transcendental"). Habermas maintains that a condition for human communication is that no matter how else they differ, interlocutors share certain presuppositions of communication, among which is a presumption that there will be a measure of mutual toleration and respect.[11] Habermas thus depicts an ideal form of discourse in which free, equal, and rational agents strive nonantagonistically to reach consensus as a standard for normative social philosophy.

Such an exposition surely does show that anyone who values trying to settle differences by means of rational discussion rather than by force ought also to favour a world that optimizes the conditions for such discussion. That it does not demonstrate that all language users *do* act in accord with this value is all too evident in the world of today (or of any other time). Whether it shows that everyone *ought* to embrace the value is a matter of ongoing philosophical debate, as are such questions as whether Habermas's scheme places unwarranted emphasis on consensus, thus unrealistically minimizing conflict and undesirably downplaying difference, or whether he uncritically reflects an ethnocentric European Enlightenment Rationalism.[12] (On the first criticism the approach would fail to address the hemlock problem; on the second, it would be another Owl of Minerva.)

PHILOSOPHY AND DEMOCRATIC PARTISANSHIP

Of the several directions the ensuing debate has taken, the most useful for the purpose of this essay might be called "democracy partisanship." In his instructive study of related controversies, Richard Bernstein notes a general difficulty. While applauding Habermas for defending democracy, Bernstein questions the security of his defence, based as it is on contested theory.[13] Of course, a Habermasian, or any other philosopher who claims to derive democratic prescriptions from philosophical principles, could agree and maintain that those who dispute their view are wrong, but this would miss the force of Bernstein's criticism.

A prodemocrat, he does not want support for democracy to depend on acceptance of a controversial philosophical theory. This is why, like Cornel West, he favours the work of John Dewey, who explicitly made his philosophical endeavours subservient to the exigencies of democratic practice.[14] Bernstein and West read Dewey as a consciously culture-bound philosopher whose culture is liberal-democratic. Their criticism of Dewey and Rorty is that their insensitivity to economic and other structural limitations on U.S. liberal democracy made their exclusively reformist, or in Rorty's case even apologetic, stances insufficient regarding democratic progress in this society itself.[15]

These misgivings are well taken; however, democratic partisanship of Rorty's variety is also subject to criticism from another direction. Defending his relativistic version of pragmatism, Rorty challenges philosophical realists by citing as now defunct "such claims as 'If God does not exist, everything is permitted,' 'Man's dignity consists in his link with a supernatural order,' and 'One must not mock holy things,'"[16] which intuitions Rorty describes as having been "weeded out from among the intellectually respectable candidates for Philosophical articulation."[17] Surely these tenets have not been "weeded out," but continue to inform the efforts of a great many of the world's philosophers, including those in Rorty's contemporary United States and I imagine in his own university. It is in recognition of the coexistence of such popularly motivating "metaphysical" viewpoints with each other and with liberal-democratic values that several contemporary political philosophers address the problem earlier set aside about liberal neutrality and pluralism. An example is Rawls.

For him, philosophy should be divided into two species: "comprehensive" philosophy, which aims at general theories of virtue or the good, and "political philosophy." The former is supposed to pursue its proper aim independently of reference to political considerations, while political philosophy attempts to recommend political arrangements that are to apply to people embracing different views about the good life. Political philosophy thus indicates which comprehensive-philosophical prescriptions fall within politically acceptable limits. Deploying his famous method, Rawls defends a version of liberal democracy within which activity in accord with any comprehensive religious or philosophical view is countenanced so long as it does not conflict with such "primary" political goods as liberal freedoms or equality of opportunity.[18]

Two, rather large modifications of Rawls's suggestion serve to explicate a variant relevant to present purposes of the prodemocratic approach to philosophy defended by Dewey, West, and Bernstein. The first modification accepts the distinction between political and comprehensive philosophy, but insists that political philosophy be made deliberately subservient to the project of making progress in democracy. Prescribed here is not that a new political philosophy be constructed (though this is not ruled out either), but just (a) that among the criteria that determine what a political philosopher considers a good reason for endorsing, for example, some definition of "freedom" or "equality," for weighting these or other values, for constructing a theory of the relation between virtue and justice, and so on, be an estimation of how far popular embrace[19] of the result would promote democracy; and (b) that among the political philosopher's criteria this one take precedence over others in the sense that it function as a necessary condition for acceptability.[20]

The second modification challenges the sharpness of a putative line between political and comprehensive philosophy. Rawls's reason for distinguishing between them is to give priority of the "right" over the "good" while leaving room for pluralistic respect for alternative visions of the latter. To be sure, Rawls's conclusion is contested, as arguments can be given both for and against this solution to what is here designated the problem of liberal neutrality,[21] but I do not think that this should count against him. Rather, as with much political theory and practice, we confront a situation where tensions among competing values is unavoidable, so the task is not, in a circle-squaring way, to attempt full resolution but to seek ways of easing the tensions. In the case of the problem of defending liberal neutrality without imposing it on recalcitrant traditions, this is achieved to the extent that the traditions of a society, those articulated in its comprehensive philosophies, themselves incorporate pluralistic values, or, as Rawls puts it, that there is an overlapping consensus on this point.[22]

Rawls's narrow concept of the realm of the political confines it to constitutional (or quasi-constitutional) governing structures: "[P]olitical virtues must be distinguished from the virtues that characterize ways of life belonging to comprehensive religious and philosophical doctrines, as well as from the virtues falling under various associational ideas (the ideals of churches and universities, occupations and vocations, clubs and teams) and those appropriate to roles in family life and the relations between individuals."[23] But when democracy is considered broadly as something that affects just such associations of people as churches, universities, vocational settings, and families—to which "comprehensive" philosophy certainly does pertain—it is appropriate to ask how far such philosophy promotes democratic self-determination in these domains.

Since this, in turn, requires a measure of internal and external tolerance,[24] the conflict between institutionalized rights and extraconstitutional goods can be minimized. The conclusion to be drawn from these considerations (now to formulate the second suggested modification of Rawls's strategy) is that the prodemocratic political philosopher ought actively to encourage incorporation of a democratic criterion also within the pursuit of philosophy generally, or at least that range of philosophy that is potentially implicated in views about how people might comport themselves in situations of ongoing interaction.[25]

The sort of democratic criterion I have in mind is stronger than one simply encouraging those holding conflicting comprehensive-philosophical conclusions to incorporate respect for democratic norms, like mutual tolerance, procedurally into their interactions as philosophical interlocutors. I doubt that procedural and substantive philosophical norms can consistently be isolated from each other. If a comprehensive philosopher can be persuaded that in the event of conflict, prescriptions derived from substantive principles should be overridden by those derived from procedural considerations, then, unless the philosopher is sloppy or insincere, this must count in favour of providing a basis (if only in the sense of leaving room) for democratic procedural prescriptions within the substance of his or her philosophical views. At the same time, the suggested criterion is weaker than a sufficient condition, and it is not even a necessary condition if this is taken to mean that exceptions are never justified.

While some philosophical traditions may lend themselves to thoroughgoing democratization, as West maintains with respect to the "prophetic pragmatism" he sees as the issue of an "Emersonian culture of creative democracy" in the United States,[26] I fear that general deployment of the democratic criterion strongly interpreted could function as a sort of democratic Lysenkoism to subordinate the pursuit of philosophy to something extraneous to it, thus limiting the freedom of innovation and the search for philosophical truth (or whatever analogue of truth is thought to make the enterprise worth undertaking). For this reason it is not here specified with respect to comprehensive philosophy that democracy be a privileged point of philosophical orientation, or even a condition admitting of no exceptions.

Rather, the prescription is that whatever other criteria are deemed appropriate in the construction, elaboration, defence, and evaluation of comprehensive philosophical theory, contributing to democracy be included in a presumptive way such that, on the one hand, there is an onus to justify its violation, while, on the other hand, appeal to it may be appropriate for overriding other criteria. (Perhaps a democratic criterion applied to specifically political philosophy could also be taken as only presumptively necessary, but carrying a heavier onus, somehow measured, to justify exceptions.)

Still, it might be maintained that political criteria have no place at all, at least in the work of comprehensive philosophers. One response to this source of resistance challenges the supposition that there are domains of philosophy which are entirely apolitical. Though in sympathy with a political-historicistic orientation often expressed in Marxist historiography, or in a different way in some of Foucault's writings, whereby a direct and intimate connection between philosophy and politics is made,[27] I think that less contestable lines of potential interaction should suffice to call into question the apolitical claim. MacIntyre puts it nicely: "[E]ven the more abstract and technical issues of our discipline—issues concerning naming, reference, truth, and translatability—may on occasion be as crucial in their political or social implications as are theories of the social contract or of natural right. The former no less than the latter have implications for the nature and limitations of rationality in the arenas of political society."[28]

Supplementing this challenge to philosophical apoliticalness are the procedural considerations alluded to above. It is clearly in the interest of philosophers, *qua* philosophers, to promote democratic pluralism. A straightforward case can be made out that promoting pluralistic tolerance and mutual respect among philosophers is advantageous to their philosophical work, as this allows them to learn from one another and to subject their views to the strongest criticism. Moreover, given that philosophical activity cannot be realistically isolated from the cultural and institutional features of a society within which it is carried out, it should make a difference to the philosopher how democratic his or her surrounding society is as well.

Neither the visionary nor the critical dimensions of philosophy are effectively pursued in an autocracy, as even philosophers whose visions happen to have been in accord with those of the autocrats sometimes find out. Philosophy which sets out to explicate and defend existing values, but which finds this job too easy because rival views are excluded a hearing, will quickly become ideological rationalization. For the utopian and the radical critic it is clearly advantageous that a level of democracy has been secured where iconoclasm and dissent are institutionally protected. Thus, given that there are advantages to democracy for the proper work of philosophers, and that they have it within their power to contribute to the protection and enhancement of democracy (albeit slightly, but without having to become philosopher kings), it would require a peculiar understanding of practical rationality not to draw the obvious conclusion.

Another criticism might challenge the amenability of all philosophical orientations to deployment of this criterion, citing the many examples of support that a variety of these orientations have given to *anti*democratic measures. The counter claim need not ignore the antidemocratic potentials of some or even all philosophies. Just as the potentiality of democratic regress in a society coexists with the potentiality for progress, with no guarantee that the latter will prevail, so philosophical theories may be carried out in more than one way. Still, it must be admitted that a general proof that any philosophical approach is potentially democratic does not come to mind, and it may be that some approaches are entirely inimical to democracy.

On the perspective enjoined here, this would count as a good *philosophical* reason to reject such an approach (though to maintain consistency, this would not sanction antidemocratic intolerance). Nonetheless, in favour of optimism is the fact that, in accord with the radically critical and therefore autocritical dimension of the philosophical enterprise as here understood, we are not dealing with frozen orientations. Also, in the case of those philosophers who can be persuaded of democratic procedural advantages, there is a point of entry for debate about the merits of democracy generally. Finally, there are examples of the democratic appropriation of otherwise quite diverse positions in philosophy: Adler's use of Aristotle, Foucault's of Nietzsche, D'Hondt's or Taylor's of Hegel, Gramsci's of Croce, and so on.

It might be allowed that any philosophical orientation admits of being democracy serving, but it could be claimed that in a society with an antidemocratic culture, such potential could not be exploited. This criticism will be less damaging for one (like Dewey or Macpherson) who sees democracy as a matter of degree than for others. On the degrees-of-democracy view, there is at least the possibility that even a society the culture of which exhibits grossly antidemocratic features may simultaneously contain prodemocratic ones as well. This means that a philosopher employing the prescribed criterion can avoid the Owl of Minerva problem in such a society by seeking out and striving to nurture its prodemocratic features; while the hemlock problem is also avoided provided such features, however marginalized, really are there to be found. What confidence can one have that this will always be the case?

A way of reading Habermas's arguments about the suppositions of a linguistic community is as an attempted general proof that all cultures are potentially democratic, and Dewey was of the opinion that human intersubjectivity was such that, as he put it, democracy is "the human condition itself."[29] Whether or not general proofs are available, it seems to me that considering what a society completely void of democracy would be like (perhaps Hades would count), the burden of proof is on the critic to adduce a political culture which contains not a shred of prodemocratic potential. This topic will be further pursued in Essay 6. I have the impression that the pessimistic opinion derives in part from thinking of democracy as such an all-or-nothing affair that when overtly antidemocratic features of a culture are perceived, it is assumed to be entirely void of democratic impulse; and in part from a narrow, and often ethnocentric, identification of democracy with whatever formal democratic structures exist in one's own society.

A final objection to democratic partisanship is philosophical. Could it not be argued that both the conception of democracy employed in this paper and the prescription to incorporate a prodemocratic criterion within the practice of philosophy are themselves part of a theory requiring philosophical justification? If so, it might be concluded, then acceptance of the democratic prescription is contingent on acceptance of whatever principles inform the philosophical theory behind it. I think of two rejoinders to this argument, a preferred, if radical, one and a safer, if boring, rejoinder.

DEMOCRACY AND THE BOUNDARIES OF PHILOSOPHY

The radical response maintains that considerations of democracy—that is, conceptions of what it is and how it is to be valued—are *extraphilosophical*. Let me summarize the two claims which in a much longer paper would require full defence to make this case: that *something* is extraphilosophical,[30] and that *democracy* is such a thing. One support for the first of these claims may be found in some of the arguments of Marxists, pragmatists, and social-scientifically oriented phenomenologists, and has been especially well articulated in recent feminist philosophy. I am thinking of those feminists who insist that philosophical, as other theoretical, labour commence by identifying the specific, actual-life situations that give rise to a philosophical problem and that guide efforts to address it.

Though there are, to be sure, alternative ways to characterize the relation between philosophical theorizing and such a "lived world," and though most who advance this view admit reciprocal interaction between the given circumstances and philosophical reflection on them, some sort of philosophy-independent status is accorded the concrete sources of philosophy. Not to recognize this independence is, the feminists rightly note, to embrace a typically male-intellectual image of thought as coming from nobody and no place.[31]

There is also the more traditionally established defence of extraphilosophicalness expressed in Rawls's notion of reflective equilibrium. Addressing political philosophy (but in a way that could be generalized to any other focus), Rawls claims that advances in thought can only be made by testing philosophical theory against everyday intuitions. This observation so patently summarizes the way that all philosophy has in fact been carried out, that Rawls's main critics have been from the side of those who wish to "widen" what is put into equilibrium with philosophical theory to include such things as empirical knowledge.[32] However, even if no more than Rawls's intuitions are admitted the place he gives them, this allows into the arena of philosophy something extraphilosophical; since if the intuitions were ultimately entirely philosophically shaped, appeal to them to advance philosophy would be futile.

A comment by Jacques Derrida suggests one way that *democracy* might be regarded among those things that are extraphilosophical. Speaking at an international conference of political philosophers, he invited those present to attend to the fact that, despite their different nationalities, politics, and philosophies, in their interaction as critical philosophers they illustrated "the form of democracy as the political milieu of every international philosophical colloquium."[33] One could expand this observation as evidence, if not proof, of the claim that democracy is extraphilosophical. In forums for the actual pursuit of philosophy, men and women with radically diverse philosophical orientations still recognize how this pursuit might be democratically carried on.[34]

A more general defence could proceed by interpreting the Deweyan thesis referred to earlier that democracy is the human condition. One elaboration might simply point out that democracy has to do with how people make collective decisions in circumstances of mutual constraint, that human action typically involves making decisions, and that individuals are always in mutually affecting social circumstances. Informal "democratic politics" will thus be such an integral part of daily life as to count as the sort of thing referred to by the Marxists, feminists, and social phenomenologists, or as appropriately appealed to in wide reflective equilibrium.

The safer rejoinder to the charge that the prescription for democratic philosophy is philosophically contentious grants that the prescription is philosophical, but denies that it is contentious. I hope that I shall be believed when I aver that I do not myself know whether or how the concept of democracy employed in this essay and the prescription for integrating a prodemocratic criterion into philosophical endeavours is philosophically derived. However, if it is, then I think it must be philosophically innocuous. That is, it ought to be at such a low level of philosophical generality that, with suitable qualification and tightening of some definitions, it is at least comprehensible to someone who thinks within any philosophical orientation, as should be the thesis that incorporation of the democratic criterion is in the interests of the philosophical profession *per se*.

Neither in the case when democracy is considered extraphilosophical nor when it is considered philosophically innocuous is it assumed that democracy is also positively valued. Arguments need to be given why people in general and philosophers in particular should favour democracy. The claim advanced here is that, to the extent that democracy is thought of as extraphilosophical, then nonphilosophical arguments should accomplish this task; while to the extent that it is regarded as philosophically innocuous, then philosophical argumentation within any (live and serious) philosophical orientation can motivate a prodemocratic conclusion. Gatherings of philosophers and interchange in philosophical publications are good forums to put this claim to the test.

AGAINST A SOCIALIST PHILOSOPHY

Earlier it was queried whether liberal-democratic theory should be considered a philosophical position at all. A ground for raising this question is that, whereas it requires argumentation to support a debatable claim that political philosophies should include the promotion of democracy as a condition for adequacy, liberal-democratic thought (nonhypocritically undertaken) explicitly puts democracy at its centre. Most of the intellectual activity of liberal democrats is devoted to the pragmatics associated with actual democratic politics. When philosophical theses are appealed to this is typically to articulate and/or to defend choices that such politics place on some society's agenda. For instance, appeal to doctrines in the philosophy of law might help to sort out and choose among options about juridic activism and, similarly, regarding rights theory and concrete issues of freedom of speech; philosophical theories of justice and taxation policy; collective decision theory and democratic electoral principles.

A second ground for the suggestion is to avoid the danger that making liberal democracy into a philosophical theory could itself be undemocratic.

Candidates for providing the core of the philosophical foundations of liberal democracy have included Locke, Mill, Kant, Rawls, and even Rousseau and Hobbes. But in virtue of the widely divergent visions of possible and desirable political arrangements embodied in the viewpoints of these philosophers, it would run counter to the open-ended, context-sensitive, and pluralistic exigencies of democratic politics to insist that one of them, or some philosophical alternative, expresses the truly liberal-democratic vision. (It might be noted that this ground for freeing liberal democracy from philosophy also applies to nonliberal-democratic political theory and practice, for instance, that which looks exclusively to facilitate collective decision making by direct participation and consensus building.)

I conclude by urging that these considerations apply to socialist theory as well. It was argued at the beginning of this essay that the component parts of official-line Marxist philosophy functioned together in such a way as embarrassingly to support authoritarian socialism. I now wish to recall the claim of Essay 2 that the *form* of this Marxism as a putatively philosophically grounded world view also contributed support. Thinking of real existing socialism as based on a philosophical world view inhibited innovation in practical political and economic activity, as, indeed, it did in science, technology, and art; and it reinforced antipluralism, for instance, in respect of religion and national cultures. To avoid repetitions of this history, I submit that socialist theory, no matter how much or little of Marxism it retains, should, like liberal-democratic theory, be made entirely subservient to democracy. Accordingly, it should not be regarded as a philosophical world view. This does not mean that distinctively socialist ideas should not be vigorously interjected into popular culture and put into political practice.

To my way of thinking, socialism should be promoted as the egalitarian moment in the project of making major advances in whatever levels of democracy exist in today's politically organized societies. While problems to which philosophical work is relevant no doubt confront the explication and defence of socialism thus conceived (as they also confront alternative conceptions of socialism), socialist theory need not be made into a general philosophical egalitarianism. Rather, socialist theorists may sometimes find it useful to draw upon relevant work in philosophy—whether political or comprehensive—especially if this has been pursued in the democracy-friendly way prescribed above. Some democratically motivated philosophers who are also socialists may resist the subservient role into which this casts them. Perhaps they will be consoled if the exchange for loss of philosophical pretence can be made into a gain in political efficacy.

Notes

1. Little is to be gained by scholastic approaches to Marxist texts undertaken by those socialists who see it as important to draw a clear line between true Marxism and true non-Marxism: Indeed such an approach was itself typical of authoritarian use of Marxism. How embarrassing official-line Marxism is to socialist theorists will depend upon how much of it they are prepared to reject completely. I can think of very few socialists who could be considered 100 percent Marx free. Perhaps Isaac Balbus would come close if he could interpret all aspects of the Marxist vision as an example of male chauvinist productivism, *Marxism and Domination* (Princeton, NJ: Princeton University Press, 1982). My own way of regarding Marxism is outlined in Essay 2 of this collection and also treated in my *Democratic Theory and Socialism* (Cambridge: Cambridge University Press, 1987), 15–16.

2. C. B. Macpherson, *The Real World of Democracy* (Toronto: Canadian Broadcasting Corporation, 1965; reprinted, Concord, Ont.: Anasi, 1992). See, too, Joshua Cohen and Joel Rogers, *On Democracy* (Harmondsworth: Penguin, 1983); Norberto Bobbio, *The Future of Democracy* (Minneapolis: University of Minnesota Press, 1987); Philip Green, *Retrieving Democracy* (Totowa, NJ: Rowman & Allenheld, 1985); Allen Buchanan, *Marx and Justice* (Totowa, NJ: Rowman & Allenheld, 1982); David Schweickart, "Should Rawls Be a Socialist?" *Social Theory and Practice*, Vol. 5, No. 1 (Fall 1978), 1–27; Jeffrey Reiman, "The Possibility of a Marxian Theory of Justice," in Kai Nielsen and Steven Patten, eds., *Marx and Morality* (Guelph, Ont.: Canadian Association for Publishing in Philosophy, 1981), 307–22.

3. Whether or how it is significant, as Fukuyama claims in his "End of History" article, first published in a recent issue of *The Public Interest* and widely reproduced and reiterated in *The Guardian* (Sept. 7, 1990), that there has not been a war between full-fledged liberal democracies is a matter for debate. That liberal democracies have waged unjustified and deeply destructive wars, overtly as in Vietnam and covertly elsewhere in the third world, is undeniable, as, for example, Noam Chomsky's documented accounts illustrate. See his *The Washington Connection and Third World Fascism*, coauthored with Edward Herman (Montreal: Black Rose Books, 1979), and *Turning the Tide: The U.S. and Latin America* (Montreal: Black Rose Books, 1986). A pertinent critique of Fukuyama is by Stephen Eric Bronner, *Moments of Decision: Political History and the Crises of Radicalism* (New York: Routledge, 1992), chap. 6.

4. Examples of antiliberal-democratic radical theorists are Andrew Levine, *Liberal Democracy: A Critique of Its Theory* (New York: Columbia University Press, 1981) and *The End of the State* (London: Verso, 1988); and Benjamin Barber, *Strong Democracy* (Berkeley: University of California Press, 1984).

5. The term "visions of the world" is used in lieu of "world views" or "fundamental vision" to allow antifoundationists to count as visionary philosophers. Nietzsche is often and appropriately cited as a philosopher who criticized the effort to construct philosophical theories on the basis of putative first principles or to

produce unified *Weltanschauungen*. Yet he projects a vision of the world; that is, there is a uniquely Nietzschean view about what constitutes a meaningful or worthwhile life, what can be known and is worth knowing, and so on. I think that the same observation applies to Wittgenstein and Derrida, though their visions of the world are best exemplified in the attitudes of those who have come to think in terms of these figures' core philosophical theses.

6. Since it is hard to find philosophers recognizing themselves as participating in such a division of labour (*except* when they design and promote their university departmental curricula, converse with nonphilosophers about their jobs, and otherwise act as everyday beings in the world), the point can be put that an image of philosophy in this full-blown way constitutes a paradigm or an ideal-typical concept, by approximation to which the practices called "philosophical" are so recognized.

7. A full treatment of "democracy" is in my *Democratic Theory*, chap. 3.

8. See Richard Rorty's essay, "Solidarity or Objectivity?" in John Rajchman and Cornel West, eds., *Post-Analytic Philosophy* (New York: Columbia University Press, 1985), 3–19, at 11–12. Amy Gutman, among others, has rightly challenged the communitarians' assumption of homogeneity of tradition within communities, "Communitarian Critics of Liberalism," *Philosophy and Public Affairs*, Vol. 14, No. 3 (Summer 1985), 308–22.

9. Alasdair MacIntyre, *Whose Justice? Which Rationality?* (Notre Dame, IN: University of Notre Dame Press, 1988), see 361–62, 387–88.

10. Michael Walzer, *The Company of Critics: Social Criticism and Political Commitment in the 20th Century* (New York: Basic Books, 1988).

11. This thesis is defended by Habermas, *Theory of Communicative Action* (Boston: Beacon Press, 1984), and related explicitly to democracy in his *Legitimation Crisis* (Boston: Beacon, 1973).

12. See a review of criticisms of Habermas's emphasis on consensus by David Rasmussen in his *Reading Habermas* (Cambridge, MA: Blackwell, 1990), 40–44, and see Rasmussen's general treatment of Habermasian ethics, chap. 4. François Lyotard's critique of Habermas's Rationalism is in *La Condition postmoderne* (Paris: Les Editions de Minuit, 1979). A sample response by Habermas is in "Modernity versus Postmodernity," *New German Critique*, Vol. 22 (1981), 3–14, and see the essays in Richard Bernstein, ed., *Habermas and Modernity* (Cambridge, MA: MIT Press, 1985).

13. See Richard Bernstein, *Philosophical Profiles* (Philadelphia: University of Pennsylvania Press, 1986), 74–76.

14. Richard Bernstein, *Praxis and Action* (Philadelphia: University of Pennsylvania Press, 1971), pt. 3, "Peirce and Dewey." Cornel West, *The American Evasion of Philosophy: A Geneology of Pragmatism* (Madison: University of Wisconsin Press, 1989), chap. 3.

15. See Bernstein's discussion of Dewey in his *Profiles*. His criticism is expressed in *Praxis and Action*, 227–29. West, *American Evasion*, criticizes Dewey at 102 and Rorty at 207.

16. Richard Rorty, "Pragmatism and Philosophy," in Kenneth Baynes, *et al.*, eds., *After Philosophy: End or Transformation?* (Cambridge, MA: MIT Press, 1989), 26–66, at 45.

17. *Ibid.*, 55. In a similarly antitolerant vein, Rorty elsewhere writes: "Either we

attach a special privilege to our own community, or we pretend an impossible tolerance for every other group." And, "We Western liberal intellectuals should accept the fact that we have to start from where we are, and that this means that there are lots of views which we simply cannot take seriously," in Rajchman and West, eds., *Post-Analytic*, 12.

18. John Rawls, "The Priority of Right and Ideas of the Good," *Philosophy and Public Affairs*, Vol. 17, No. 4 (1988), 251-76; and "Justice as Fairness: Political not Metaphysical," *Philosophy and Public Affairs*, Vol. 17, No.3 (1985), 223-51, both revised in his *Political Liberalism* (New York: Columbia University Press, 1993).

19. Inclusion of the notion of "popular embrace" does not mean that a philosophical theory must pass a popularity test or the like; this certainly would call out the Owl of Minerva. Philosophical views may challenge popular opinion with an eye to changing it, and this change need not be direct and immediate. On the other hand, the prescribed criterion does entail a Gramsci-like admonition that philosophy be made relevant to people's concerns and pursued in such a way as to have potential impact on popular culture.

20. I imagine such a criterion being integrated with, rather than added to, the main focus of a political philosopher's attention. Thus, for example, a philosopher primarily motivated to intepret the virtues and to prescribe that political measures be taken to instil them in the citizenry should think of how this can be done in such a way that democracy is promoted as well. Or, taking one of Rawls's criteria for an adequate theory of justice, that it show how institutions of justice would create psychological assent to themselves, *Theory of Justice* (Cambridge, MA: Harvard University Press, 1971), secs. 29, 75, 76, employment of the democratic criterion would, in the first instance, require showing how this can be done in a democratic way (i.e., nonpaternalistically, with full information and educational opportunities and through transparent means, as opposed to in a brainwashing way) and, secondly, how the auto-entrenchment of a sense of justice could be integrated with comparable prodemocratic values.

21. See the useful examination of this question by William Galston, "Pluralism and Social Unity," *Ethics*, Vol. 99, No. 4 (July 1989), 711–26.

22. Rawls, "The Idea of an Overlapping Consensus," *Oxford Journal of Legal Studies*, Vol. 7 (1987), 1-25; *Political Liberalism*, Lecture IV.

23. Rawls, "Priority," 263. The list in *Political Liberalism*, 137, is shorter.

24. A pertinent argument that toleration of minorities within a community is in the interests of community democracy is offered by Felix Oppenheim, "Democracy: Characteristics Included and Excluded," *The Monist*, Vol. 55, No. 1 (January 1971), 29–50; and Essay 6 of the present collection pursues the topic further. It is in virtue of considerations such as Oppenheim's that I think tolerance and the protection of individual rights ought not to be seen as antagonistic to democracy but as preconditions for its protection and expansion.

25. Of course one way that political philosophers might do this is by venturing into "comprehensive" philosophical terrain themselves, as Galston, "Pluralism and Social Unity," urges. In a comparable vein, Jean Hampton suggests in a thoughtful treatment of this subject that there are limits to how far political philosophers can restrict themselves to a defence of procedural respect for democratic rights, so they should defend tolerance both procedurally and philosophically, "Should Political Philosophy Be Done without Metaphysics?" *Ethics*, Vol. 99,

No. 4 (July 1989) 791–814, see 804. For reasons given below, I think that one can produce arguments in favour of including prodemocratic principles within a comprehensive-philosophical position without exactly "doing metaphysics" oneself.

26. West, *American Evasion*, 210, 239.

27. "[The term 'government' should] not cover only the legitimately constituted forms of political or economic subjection, but also modes of action, more or less considered and calculated, which were designed to act upon the possibilities of action and of other people. To govern . . . is to structure the possible field of actions of others." "The Subject and Power," in H. Dreyfus and P. Rabinow, *Michel Foucault: Beyond Structuralism and Hermeneutics* (Chicago: University of Chicago Press, 1983), 221.

28. Alasdair MacIntyre, "Relativism, Power, and Philosophy," in Kenneth Baynes, *et al.*, eds., *After Philosophy*, 385–411, at 398.

29. See Dewey's *The Public and Its Problems* (Denver, CO: Alan Swallow, 1957), 148 and *passim*.

30. To affirm that a belief is extraphilosophical is not to deny that it may be theory laden. Quite likely, any idea pertaining to such matters as how people may extend control over their lives presupposes at least commonsense theories, and it may even be that such theories are or have been objects of philosophical dispute. However, it is an undefended prejudice of some philosophers that any theory-laden belief is itself a philosophical one. Perhaps this results from assuming that any proposition that becomes or may become an object of philosophical reflection thereby becomes itself a philosophical proposition.

31. Representative expressions of this position may be found in Margaret Eichler's *The Double Standard* (London: Croom Helm, 1980), and Dorothy Smith, "A Sociology from Women," in Julia Sherman and Evelyn Beck, eds., *The Prism of Sex: Essays in the Sociology of Knowledge* (Madison: The University of Wisconsin Press, 1979), 135–87. A similar criticism of political-theoretical "universalism" is advanced by Seyla Benhabib, who resists the universalistic treatment of moral selves as "disembedded and disembodied," "The Generalised and the Concrete. Other," in Seyla Benhabib and Drucilla Cornell, eds., *Feminism as Critique* (Minneapolis: University of Minnesota Press, 1987), 77–95.

32. See Norman Daniels, "Reflective Equilibrium and Archimedean Points," *Canadian Journal of Philosophy*, Vol. 10, No. 1 (March 1980), 83–103.

33. Jacques Derrida, "The Ends of Man," in Baynes, *et al.*, eds., 125–58, at 129.

34. Democratic pursuit of philosophy in this context means such banal things as abiding by majority vote at philosophy association business meetings and refraining in less formal situations, for example, in the classroom or in editorial work, from trying to shut those with different conceptions of philosophy out of the discipline. The relevance of this observation to the current argument is that if, in their interactions with one another over and above the articulation of philosophical positions, philosophers can recognize how these and other democratic standards can govern their interactions (even if not all do in fact abide by them), then they are capable also of appealing to democratic standards in constructing and evaluating philosophical positions themselves.

ESSAY 6

Community, Democracy, and Socialism

Recent communitarian critics of individualism challenge both the liberal democrat, for embracing a pernicious and false atomic individualism, and the radical socialist, for being insensitive to community tradition. While it may once have been fashionable for socialists to dismiss such criticisms as Burke-like defences of political conservatism, this is now a dubious response, as they are currently raised by theorists such as Charles Taylor or Michael Walzer, who place themselves on the left. Moreover, a democratic socialist *ought* not to dismiss the communitarian view, since, as argued in Essay 5, it, no less than the rival individualist position, responds to a democratic imperative.

As will shortly be seen, the communitarian/individualist controversy already presents one with a tangled conceptual web before socialism is introduced. Nonetheless, I believe that progress can be made in situating socialism with respect to this controversy, and that this can be accomplished short of defending basic theories of social ontology or political epistemology. Central to the effort is partial displacement of the debate between communitarians and individualists from theoretical terrain to that of practical democratic politics. Aided by some conceptual flowcharts and consistent with one feature of

A version of this essay was published in *Praxis International*, Vol. 11, No. 3 (October 1991), and yet earlier versions were read in 1988 at The A. E. Havens Center, University of Wisconsin, and in 1989 at the Centro Piero Gobetti, Turin, and the Departments of Philosophy, University of Naples and University of Amsterdam. I have profited from criticisms by Nicola Badaloni, Veit Bader, Norberto Bobbio, Dominico Jervolino, Costanzo Preve, Mario Reale, and Svetozar Stojanović.

"middle-range," in contrast to foundational, philosophy I shall also indicate both the scope and the limitations of the essay's conclusions.

CRITICAL COMMUNITARIANISM

While strongly advocating that community traditions merit protection, the theorists with whom this essay is concerned do not thereby endorse conservative traditionalism. On Chart 6.1 they may be located as critical protective communitarians, who unlike the conservatives, believe that a prescription to protect traditions is compatible with taking a critical attitude toward them. At the same time, with the conservatives, they are to be distinguished from constructive communitarians, who, like Rousseau and often in his name, centrally prescribe that new communities embodying the values they favour be brought into existence.[1] Since this, too, seems to me important, I hope the conclusions of

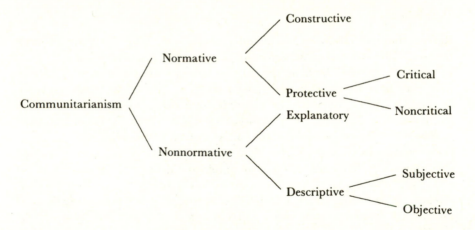

CHART 6.1

this essay can contribute to the task (not undertaken in it) to show how critical-protective and constructive communitarianisms might be compatible.

Nor are the communitarians in question to be confused with those socialists, like Adam Przeworski or Richard Miller, who, in different ways, attempt to integrate a nonnormative theory of class-based communities with an approach to social explanation.[2] Rather, they are concerned with normative matters, though they must presuppose some criteria in virtue of which communities may be identified. While this task is not without problems, it is still relatively straightforward for the communitarians insofar as they describe communities in terms of the subjective perception of their members, rather than in the manner of those Marxists who, for example, think of class-based communities objectively.[3]

These classificatory points are made not just to locate the communitarian position, but to indicate the relative narrowness of its scope. Being primarily normative, the position does not commit one to very much in the way of substantive social theory, and is therefore compatible with a variety of approaches to social science. Even as a normative perspective, the position cannot be a full-blown ethical theory, since, to the extent that it is critical, it must allow for exceptions to its core community-supporting prescription.

One shortcoming in communitarian literature is a failure to define "community." A full definition would no doubt be difficult to produce. A crucial component to any definition, however, must be a link between the notion of community and that of tradition. I take it that whatever other conditions something should satisfy properly to be called a "community," it must be such that (a) there are certain circumstances, for example, being of a common nationality, class, or ethnicity, or having been raised within a common religious tradition, which its members find themselves sharing (rather than having invented the circumstances themselves), and at least partly by reference to which they identify themselves; and (b) among these circumstances are traditionally held beliefs with generally understood noninstrumental normative implications regarding domains of behaviour appropriate to the shared circumstances of community members in their ongoing life.

The term "noninstrumental" is employed to capture the idea that the norms are perceived by community members as ones which obligate behaviour in accord with them rather than as useful means to attaining other goals (as for example, in the case of the instrumental norms of proper behaviour in impersonal market transactions). The qualification about "ongoing life" is meant to indicate that, being implicated in people's sense of their own identity, norms are always part of common sense and hence of the daily life of community members. While in a premodern era communities were typically regionally localized and neighbourhoods were composed of relatively homogeneous coextensive clusters of communities, this definition departs from some standard ones in not laying down shared spatial territory as a conceptually necessary condition for something to be a community.[4] This abstention allows one to talk of religious or class-constituted communities cutting across local frontiers. A fuller definition would require specifying the sorts of circumstances that must be shared and laying down criteria to determine what counts as being "appropriate" to a circumstance thus shared. Perhaps this obligation can be sidestepped for present purposes.

At the base of the communitarian's central prescription is the view expressed in this often-quoted passage from Alisdair MacIntyre's *After Virtue*:

> [W]e all approach our own circumstances as bearers of a particular
> social identity. I am someone's son or daughter, someone else's cousin
> or uncle; I am a citizen of this or that city, a member of this or that guild
> or profession; I belong to this clan, that tribe, this nation. Hence what is
> good for me has to be the good for one who inhabits these roles. As such
> I inherit from the past of my family, my city, my tribe, my nation, a
> variety of debts, inheritances, rightful expectations and obligations.
> This constitutes the given of my life, my moral starting point. This is in
> part what gives my life its own moral particularity.[5]

MacIntyre's conclusion is that those outside of a community should likewise respect the norms its own members recognize. Defence of this prescription typically involves an element of "ought implies can" argumentation, but it obviously cannot appeal entirely to inevitability. If people were not capable of pursuing goods other than those embodied in their traditional roles, there would be no need for communitarian injunctions at all.

Rather, most communitarians probably endorse the claim of Walzer that political philosophizing that seeks to explicate and order the values which communities of people already have—philosophizing that remains within Plato's cave, as Walzer nicely puts it—is more realistic and practical than more abstract efforts, while recognizing the possibility of alternatives.[6] Indeed, a main thrust of communitarianism has been to attack rival efforts for reinforcing modern amoralism and isolation.[7] At the same time, communitarians try to exhibit the positive benefits of their approach, in the way for example, that MacIntyre links respect for traditional values with the virtues[8] or that Taylor endorses Hegelian *Sittlichkeit* as necessary to avoid the alienation of atomistic individualism.[9]

We thus have two sorts of argument in favour of normative communitarianism: (a) that it accords with the fact that people are unavoidably the product of their social interactions, the most pervasive and intimate of which are community based; and (b) that respect for community fosters virtue and avoids alienation. To these, we might now add two more arguments found in communitarian texts, one philosophical and one political; namely (c) that the alternative to communitarianism would be an ethical theory appealing to some standard other than the values people have given themselves, but there are no good reasons to believe that philosophers will ever find this "Archimedean point" which has so far eluded them;[10] and (d) that to reject the communitarian prescription is to embrace a dangerously antidemocratic paternalism.[11]

SOCIALIST APPROACHES

Is the communitarian perspective as just summarized one that a socialist could accept? In broad outline at least some of the communitarian arguments are ones that socialists themselves have advanced. Most socialists probably agree with Marx's famous comment in his *Theses on Feuerbach* that "the individual is the ensemble of his social relations," at least interpreted to mean that people are crucially shaped by their historically embedded social circumstances,[12] and they, too, deplore the alienation and egoism that pervade modern life. While there no doubt are some Cartesian socialists, most harbour a historicistic mistrust of theories based on putative first principles. Similarly, while some socialists may still endorse paternalistic political practices, most have surely learned where paternalistic socialism leads. Despite these similarities, however, it has been my experience that when the merits of communitarianism are debated, at least in North American socialist circles, it is more often than not resisted on the grounds that it ignores or denigrates class struggle.[13]

The distinctions noted in Chart 6.2 (which supplement distinctions in earlier essays and come at the conceptualization of socialism more abstractly than they) will help to indicate some of the complexities involved in evaluating this charge. The complaint is usually voiced by those for whom the principal task of socialist theory is to advance the interests of the working class, either to gain working-class political power or workers' control of workplaces or both. However, pursuit of such theory involves several dimensions and may be carried on in a variety of ways, not all of which are incompatible with communitarianism.

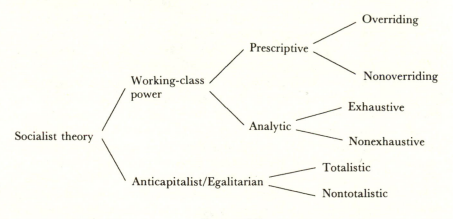

CHART 6.2

A socialist theorist thus motivated will be concerned both to analyse society and (unless the theorist is a thoroughgoing fatalist) to make prescriptions for social action, where the first task appeals to the dynamics of class struggle, and the second to what is required to advance working-class interests. Such socialist theory may be more or less "austerely" pursued in respect of each task. The austere socialist insists that promoting working-class interests must always override any other consideration and advances class-struggle-based analyses as exhaustive of social reality. Now, communitarianism was described above as a normative position, whose appeal to social analysis requires only that one can identify communities; hence, abstractly regarded, it is only in conflict with a normative class-based theory which yields overriding prescriptions.

The same point can be made about an approach to socialist theory (that may coincide with a working-class-power oriented one, but, as was argued in Essays 3 and 4, need not) in which the principal aim is to replace a predominantly capitalist economy with one that promotes certain kinds of equality. Though not marked on the chart, this sort of socialist theory also admits of analytic and normative conduct, and it may be austerely pursued by insisting that anticapitalist activity must always take precedence and by analysing every significant aspect of a society with a capitalist economy as an effect or an aspect of capitalism. I have used the current term "totalistic" to describe this version of anticapitalist socialist theorizing. Here again, socialist theory need be in contradiction with communitarianism only insofar as totalistic socialist prescription is concerned.

Indeed, it is even logically possible that communitarianism is not in contradiction to every version of austere approaches to socialist theory. One can imagine austere class-partisan theorists who specify that their prescriptions pertain to the working class only objectively regarded and who appeal Hegel-like to the cunning of reason to show that these prescriptions always coincide with community interests. Or an anticapitalist theorist could maintain that defence of community traditions always works against capitalism. The point of these observations is to show that communitarianism and socialist theory are not automatically at odds and that therefore socialists should not jump to this conclusion. At the same time, by sketching what would be required to make communitarianism compatible with austere socialism it surely becomes obvious that there are tensions.

Only an austere socialist theorist who was thinking backwards from a commitment to make his or her theory acceptable to the communitarians could arrive at such strained positions. No communitarian could rest easy with an approach in which respect for any of a community's traditions depended on showing that this is in accord with putative class interests or contributes to the defeat of capitalism, and few austere socialists would be prepared to presume this compatibility. In this essay, I shall accordingly confine myself to the nonaustere versions of socialism, taking it that austere socialist theory is an orientation to the social world that has been proven pernicious and detrimental to socialist aims themselves.

Rejecting austere socialist theory does not by itself ensure compatibility between socialism and communitarianism. The socialist critic of communitarianism might recall that at least the left communitarians wish to retain room for criticisms of traditions and then, noting the paucity of criteria to guide criticism in communitarian literature, advance a socialist criterion for *sorting* traditions into those which are worthy of retention and those which should be combatted. Thus, one who rejects totalistic (or overriding or exhaustive) approaches to socialist theory might nonetheless claim that, regarding community tradition (if not regarding all other social facts), pro-working-class or anticapitalist considerations are the appropriate ones by which to effect such sorting.

Whether this alternative establishes compatibility with communitarianism will depend on whether communitarians are prepared to accept socialist criteria in the evaluation of all traditions, but this seems most unlikely. Even those left communitarians who are also socialists would surely be justified in rejecting the assumption that socialist criteria are *always* the ones to which to turn as practically equivalent to the austere socialist approach.

CRITIQUE OF TRADITION

The above considerations lead to the inconclusive result that, while there are both affinities and tensions between the orientations of the left communitarians and socialists, the latter cannot obviously either incorporate or subordinate communitarianism: An appropriate stance is yet to be found. It will serve this purpose to set aside for the moment specifically socialist responses to communitarianism and look instead at responses on the part of left *individualist* critics. I am thinking here of such critics as Amy Gutman and Will Kymlicka, who criticize the communitarians for leaving no room for individuals to challenge the traditions of their communities.

Gutman charges the communitarians with harbouring the simplistic view that individuals are homogeneously shaped by single traditions, rather than by the several, sometimes conflicting, traditions that affect one's identity.[14] Kymlicka argues that communitarianism leaves no room for individual freedom in the face of the weight of tradition.[15] Of the several dimensions of these and other individualists' aptly raised criticisms, the one I wish to focus on is that communitarians provide no space for subjecting traditions to radical critique. I take this to be the core of the problems identified by the individualists, and it is also a criticism communitarianism socialists share.

Communitarians, themselves, are not unaware of the problem. I find two sorts of responses, both articulated by MacIntyre in his most recent book, *Whose Justice? Which Rationality?* One of his arguments is that "at any point it may happen to any tradition-constituted inquiry that by its own standards of progress it ceases to make progress," thus precipitating an "epistemological crisis" and forcing change.[16] A second argument is that at any time one may encounter and learn the concepts of an "alien tradition" from which "the limitations, incoherences, and poverty of resources of their own beliefs" can be identified.[17] One could examine these defences of the compatibility of respect for tradition philosophically, for example, by seeking MacIntyre's grounds for thinking traditions must incorporate a criterion of progress or by probing his conception of "alien tradition." However, I would like to suggest that this is not required to reject his alternatives, since this can be done by reflecting on their political implications. Thus, it is at this point that political displacement of a philosophical problem might help to make some progress in its solution.

Consider somebody who accepted MacIntyre's claim about traditions containing criteria of progress. Such a person might be nothing but a scholar of traditions, content to study the criteria of progress and other features of their internal structures. Such a person is of no concern to us, unless or until his or her studies lead to some actual course of action. On the other hand, it is pertinent to speculate about how the student of communities who is also an active social critic, such as those in the "company of critics" described by Michael Walzer,[18] might react to MacIntyre's theory in respect to whatever communities they, themselves, inhabit.

It is true that such a person could always be on the lookout for stresses in a tradition so as to challenge it. But it would also be an appropriate response either to explain away anomalies (as accidents or the result of the machinations of evil forces) or to modify the tradition so as to make it necessarily progressive. This is not an imaginary possibility, but an unfortunately commonly encountered phenomenon, for instance in the form of religious or political dogmatism. In fact, would this not be a more likely orientation?

MacIntyre's second solution to the problem of how communitarians can accommodate critical change in a tradition is to claim that this happens when alien traditions are encountered. However, this solution courts the same political dangers as the one just discussed, since encountering an alien tradition is one type of anomaly for the invaded tradition. And there is an additional problem. Somebody within one tradition who encounters a rival tradition might be regarded as having three global choices: to agree to disagree and keep distance, to fight, or to switch. MacIntyre's perspective renders the first option useless for his purposes, which are to explain how traditions might change, and there is reason to be sceptical about his own anticipation of the third option. At least as likely is that aliens are considered dangerous foes to be driven away or obliterated.

TRADITION AND DEMOCRACY

The strategy of the above argument was to show that the practical effects of actually adopting MacIntyre's ways of making communitarianism compatible with critique of tradition could well have effects counter to his intended purposes. Now I wish to sketch a positive argument to show that, without rejecting the plausible reasons communitarians give for their position, traditions can be effectively challenged, not in theory, but in actual political practice. Required is something that can mediate, so to speak, between radical critique and respect for tradition. Democratic practices and attitudes—understood in a generic way as pertaining to how people may collectively determine life environments they share—have two features that make them uniquely suited for such mediation.

First, as discussed in the last essay, democracy simultaneously requires both respect for tradition and the active promotion of critical attitudes toward traditional values. The former of these requirements is sometimes underemphasized by democratic theorists, who quite rightly resist the antidemocratic features of many of the world's traditions. At the same time, any sincere democrat must appreciate the importance of avoiding paternalistic practices whereby people's wills are thwarted in the name of democracy. Paternalism thus construed has a way of entrenching itself, as paternalists must sustain institutions blocking people whose values they criticize from being able effectively to participate in collective decisions, and they can rationalize this to themselves on putatively democratic grounds. However, if democracy requires a presumptive respect for the ability of people to make their shared social environments conform to their subjectively held values, then the democrat must also recognize that these values will often be the ones embodied in traditions.

At the same time, the democrat should recognize that such respect pertains to only one of the requirements for ongoing democracy. Taken alone it is compatible with the orientation of conservative communitarians like

Michael Oakeshott, for whom "politics is the activity of attending to the general arrangements of a collection of people who, in respect of their common recognition of a manner of attending to its arrangements, compose a single community."[19] The problem is the one Gutman raises about the multiplicity of traditions. Assuming that any individual will not only be acquainted with a variety of traditions, but will unavoidably be thus acquainted, insofar as his or her identity is not likely to have been formed entirely by just one hegemonic tradition, then some stance is required toward alternative traditions. Of course, intolerance is always possible (though difficult to sustain when this would require schizophrenia), but intolerance is clearly not in the interests of democracy.

A controversial, but in my view nonetheless supportable, claim of democrats is that democracy in some society is incompatible with antidemocratic behaviour on its part toward other societies. As Engels put it, "a nation cannot become free and at the same time continue to oppress other nations,"[20] and the point applies to any other type of communal entity. The democrat's claim here is that external democratic tolerance is required to make levels of democracy attained in a society secure and to facilitate future democratic progress.

In brief, the ground for this is that extending the breadth and depth of freedom in one community requires democracy internal to that community, but intolerance toward other communities breeds habits and institutions inimical to this goal. In turn, tolerance toward the traditions of others requires a critical attitude toward one's own. Attitudes of intolerance, no more than any other attitudes that can pervade a community of people, are not always foreign intruders into the traditions of that community, but they are often themselves interwoven with these traditions. Hence it is in the interests of one who values the preservation of those aspects of his or her traditions compatible with community-wide democracy to reflect on other aspects which defeat this aim.

At this point one can imagine the objection that many if not all traditions are too tightly closed to respond to democratic pressures, and hence it is unrealistic to think that they may accommodate the required measure of crictical reflection. One popular response on the part of democrats is to describe democracy itself as a tradition which is at the core of a unique community.[21] However, as noted in Essay 3, it is one thing to value democracy and another to perceive democracy as an end in itself. The latter is required to think of democracy as a community-constituting tradition, but there are reasons not to adopt this perspective. Among other difficulties, such a perception is in danger of counterposing the envisaged democratic community to other traditions, when what is required is to promote the integration of democratic values with the traditions of all communities.

This brings us to a second cluster of general features of democracy that suits it as a mediator between radical critique and a tradition-sensitive perspective. One of these is that democracy, at least as I, following Macpherson on this point, think it should be regarded, is highly context sensitive. It should be thought of as a matter of the alternative ways that groups of people, including communities, might collectively determine themselves; those ways that involve the greatest number of people (ideally everyone) in such determination are to be preferred from the point of view of democracy. Implicated in this conception is the claim, explicated in Essay 3 among other places, that democracy is a matter of degree and that it need not be foreign to any society of people whose interactions are sufficiently mutually affecting and ongoing to warrant concern over how such interaction might take place.[22] Indeed, like John Dewey, I am inclined to think that a measure of democracy is essential for any ongoing human collectivity.[23]

If democracy is a matter of degree, then things that are (more or less) democratic will be processes in respect to their measure of democracy. That is, even leaving aside the question of whether there are upper limits to how democratic this or that sort of collective can or should become, there is the possibility that something that is slightly democratic may, under the right conditions, be made much more democratic. This, in turn, means that even a modicum of democracy in a community has the potential for being expanded. This should give the democrat cause for realistic optimism. One is not faced with an all-or-nothing situation, and an already existing level of democracy or some modestly achieved level may serve as the base for making democratic advances. Among other things, this means that as people come to appreciate the several benefits of doing things in democratic ways (as the democrat claims they will)[24] they should become increasingly disposed to develop and exercise the critical skills required for secure and persisting democracy.

NATIVE WOMEN AND MENNONITES

The process of democracy as I have described it is a self-advancing one: Some democracy is required to generate more democracy. This leaves the position open to the sceptical claim that there can never be any significant level of democracy because democracy requires itself as its own necessary condition. Since I think this charge more damning in theory than in practice, perhaps I will be permitted to adduce some examples from recent experiences in my own country.

One of these concerns a major struggle of native women on some of the Indian reserves in Northern Canada to secure equal status with native men in their tribes. One issue around which this has been debated concerns a law, supported by native men, whereby a native woman, unlike a native man, who married a nonnative thereby lost native status. Native women, supported by nonnative Canadian feminists, and arguing on explicitly democratic grounds, have now won the campaign to repeal this law (though, having been turned down by Canada's Supreme Court, they were obliged to turn to the United Nations to gain their victory), and are now attending to native men's continuing support for the discriminatory practice the law reinforced.[25]

The feature of this example pertinent to our current concern is that, while the women's success will have effectively challenged a deeply entrenched dimension of native culture, namely its male chauvinism, the native women have not been arguing their case on antitraditional grounds. Quite to the contrary, their aim is to ensure that all native women can retain their community links. Moreover, while some of their nonnative supporters may have viewed native culture as irretrievably sexist, the native women themselves, like most of their supporters, partly argued their case on traditionalist grounds when they maintained that sex-based discrimination within their communities was divisive of community life and at odds with an otherwise communal native ethic. This example is meant to illustrate the way that progress in democracy in a community can lead to critique of some aspects of its traditions without being destructive of the community.

A second example pertains to intercommunity relations. During the Second World War, Canadians of Japanese ancestry had their possessions confiscated by the government of the day and were incarcerated (until 1947) on the officially given grounds, now proven both false and known to be false by the government at the time, that they constituted a fifth-column threat. It was only in 1988, after a long struggle, that they won a formal governmental apology and partial compensation.[26] During this struggle, most of Canada's many ethnic minority communities supported the Japanese-Canadian cause. Since some of these communities also have (just) grievances against the government, one might explain this as a self-interested effort to form political alliances. Such an explanation contains only partial truth, but it does not apply to Canada's Mennonite communities, which, with several others, came to the defence of the Japanese Canadians without having anything to gain by so doing.

Among the possessions seized were farm lands that the government sold off at bargain prices, some of which had been purchased by Mennonite farmers. This occasioned a debate within the Mennonite community the conclusion of which was that it was unjust and out of accord with Mennonite values that the Japanese Canadians should have been treated as they were and that some form of recompense was required. The recompense that the Mennonites themselves provided was to set up scholarship funds so that Japanese-Canadian youths could acquire university education. A striking feature of this example is that, as recognized by the Mennonites, Japanese Canadians place a higher value on university education than does the Mennonite community itself. Here we have an example of consistent adherence to a democracy-related value in one community leading to support of another community, even though the latter exhibited different traditions. On the assumption that what is actual is possible, this and the previous example are meant to support the democrat's claim to political realism.

SUPERSESSION

The argument so far has been that while there is no doubt a tension between the communitarian prescription to respect community traditions and the radical's defence of tradition-challenging critical thought, these things can both be maintained as complementary parts integral to practical activity carried out in democracy-enhancing ways. This approach is one instance of "supersessionism" to employ the terminology of Chart 6.3.

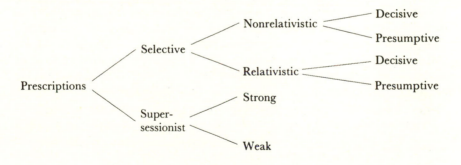

CHART 6.3

Confronted with a problematic choice, the supersessionist thinks of a social, economic, or other state of affairs in which a choice would not need to be made (that is, where one can have it both ways) and prescribes that people take appropriate actions to bring this state of affairs to pass. Thus, some socialist communitarians in the Rousseauean tradition referred to above think that in the right kind of society freedom and equality will never be in conflict; or again, some socialists claim that in a world of material abundance and without classes, social conflicts will cease to exist altogether. Austere socialist theory, as described earlier, is a species of strong supersessionism according to which after working-class power has been secured or capitalism finally defeated, oppressive dimensions of traditions will entirely atrophy, since communities are all expressions or effects of classes or class interests.

Unlike these examples, however, democratic displacement as envisaged here is of the "weak" variety. A weak supersessionist argument differs from a strong one in promising only that in the right circumstances choices will be *easier* to make than at present. Thus the democrat maintains that by making democratic progress both internal to communities and regarding their interactions, the tension between respect for tradition and critical challenge to tradition can be made increasingly less severe, even if it is never altogether eliminated. If choices must still be made, then extrasupersessionist prescriptions cannot be avoided. But such prescriptions may be more or less final. The distinction between decisive and presumptive prescriptions on the chart is meant to allow for exception-permitting prescriptions. (Relativism and antirelativism are included to indicate that the distinction between presumptive and decisive prescriptions cuts across this standard distinction in ethical theory.)

When the democrat prescribes in favour, for example, of mutual tolerance among a society's communities, this is meant to create a strong presumption in favour of tolerance. Some communities—one thinks of such as the Ku Klux Klan—are such that the presumption might be legitimately overridden. When debate with moral dimensions is carried on in the context of actual social practice, I have the impression that presumptive prescriptions almost always suffice, since it is usually possible to secure an agreement, short of winning everybody over to a common philosophical viewpoint.

It might be argued that if one can sometimes fail thus to find accord, then recourse to deep philosophical theory, yielding decisive prescriptions, is required. I am not unsympathetic to such a claim, but I would like to think that one is driven to deep philosophical debate only at the limits of democratic supersession, that is, in situations extraordinarily poor in options.[27] Philosophers who, in agreement with the prescriptions of the last essay, pursue their work in a democracy-enhancing way can, in fact, help to widen the domain wherein uniquely philosophical labour is thus unnecessary. (Enough hard cases surely exist that the philosopher is not in danger of thereby being put out of work altogether.)

SOCIALISM AND COMMUNITARIANISM

We are now in a position to return to the question set aside earlier of how socialism fits into this picture. Paralleling the different orientations of socialist theory, "socialism" admits of several interpretations, and hence there is no unique answer to this question. Socialism in the present work is regarded as a postcapitalist society, the economy of which is structured to favour equality of certain ranges and degrees of material benefits and burdens (explicated in Essays 4 and 8). Socialism may also be regarded as a movement primarily aiming to overcome working-class oppression, for which purpose the defeat of capitalism is correctly considered essential. Totalistic or exhaustive interpretations of either of these yields an austere conception of socialism, which, according to its champions, offers a strong supersessionist solution to the tradition/critique problem. Among the reasons to reject this once-popular view is that its reductionistic theory promotes sectarian, paternalistic, and other practices detrimental to democracy and to efforts to secure socialism itself. However, it still does not suffice simply to regard socialism nontotalistically or nonexhaustively. What must be added is a determination to pursue socialist politics, however socialism is conceived, in a way that subordinates it to the project of expanding democracy.

It is most unfortunate that, seizing on comments in Lenin's criticism of Kautsky or Marx's critique of the Lassalleans, and counting on a religious attitude toward Marxist texts, this opinion has in too many places and for too long a time been portrayed as antirevolutionary and otherwise suspect. To reiterate a point made in other essays of this collection, a central task for contemporary socialists is to regain a perspective wherein socialism is to be valued as an indispensable means for making radical advances in democracy.

Thus regarded, the aim of the socialist is to pursue democracy-enhancing politics—both in specifically working-class contexts and in arenas involving the interaction of other social groups, including communities, both in informal local or mass political forums, as well as in government-related politics—in such a way as to win people from increasing numbers of social domains to prosocialist commitment. This project will have succeeded with respect to the problem addressed in this essay to the extent that members of communities who wish simultaneously to criticize aspects of community tradition and to respect their own and others' traditions come to recognize both the advantages of democracy for achieving this and the advantages of socialism for democracy.[28]

LATE SOCIALISM

The history of late socialism provides an ambiguous example about the feasibility of such politics. Against the charge of individualists that communitarianism is essentially conservative, some communitarians counter that individualistic anomie is partially responsible for totalitarianism.[29] On the perspective of this paper, the unfortunate history of socialist authoritarianism substantiates *both* claims. Illiberal practices withheld preconditions for nurturing critique, such as freedom of speech. Far from replacing national, ethnic, and religious communities with a new "constructed" socialist community, the authoritarian assault on civil society drove traditions underground into privatized and isolated niches, thus strengthening their most conservative sides. The means for negotiating conflict (which was supposed to have been strongly superseded) were either disallowed or perversely maintained, and it was regarded as impossible both to be a socialist and to have strong traditional community allegiances.

From this perspective, it is not hard to explain why the democratic *potentials* of socialism were not realized. The challenge is to suggest how these potentials can be rescued from the damages authoritarianism has inflicted on socialism. This is not the place to advance concrete recommendations, nor, let it be confessed, do I feel competent to do so. One generic prescription is that space and, where necessary, protection be provided by the state, on the one hand, for communities in conflict to negotiate with one another without subordinating themselves to supra- or supercommunity goals and, on the other hand, for prodemocratic members of a community to encourage critical attitudes on the part of its members.

CONCLUSION

The advantage I claim for the methodology and prescriptions of this essay is that they focus debate on the pragmatics of democratic-socialist activity in a way that is theoretically motivated, if not by reference to fundamental philosophical principles, at least sufficiently to avoid *ad hoc*ness. In this spirit, the essay has attempted to displace the problem put before the socialist by the left communitarians onto the practical terrain of democratic-socialist politics. Those who find the prospect of such politics doomed to failure will remain sceptical that this effort at weak supersession has succeeded. A further parameter on the argument is that it primarily addresses critical normative communitarians and nonaustere socialists.

In the hope, then, that the essay's conclusion is addressed to more people than just its author, it can be put as this (presumptive) prescription: The communitarian ought, with respect to the communities he or she addresses, to encourage both respect for and critique of their traditions (therefore favouring democracy and to this end also favouring socialist equality); and the socialist should wed anticapitalist politics to democracy, and therefore embrace a respect for community traditions as well as encourage radical critique.

Notes

1. A recent example is Andrew Levine's *The End of the State* (London: Verso, 1988). Levine and I have criticized each other's views in ways bearing on this topic in the *Canadian Journal of Philosophy*, Vol. 19, No. 3 (September 1989). In his defence of individualism, Allen Buchanan admits that community is an important human good and that participation in communities is important for individuals, but he challenges as proto-totalitarian a view "advanced or at least strongly suggested" by communitarians valuing communal participation in the state, "Assessing the Communitarian Critique of Liberalism," *Ethics*, Vol. 99, No. 4 (July 1989), 852–82. It is not clear to me that the left communitarians suggest this value. They wish to protect the relative freedom of communities from one another and from the state (to which end, Buchanan notes, they should favour the rights typically championed by individualists [858]); and indeed Taylor opines that calls for the realization of a general will result from the breakdown of traditions, *Hegel* (Cambridge: Cambridge University Press, 1975), 411. The sort of communitarian criticized by Buchanan here is rather of the socialist-constructivist variety discussed below.

2. In the essay "Proletariat into a Class," in his *Capitalism and Social Democracy* (Cambridge: Cambridge University Press, 1985), Adam Przeworski prescribes giving nondeterministic accounts of class formation in a way that would make classes communities as here conceived. In *Analyzing Marx: Morality, Power and History* (Princeton, NJ: Princeton University Press, 1984), Richard Miller describes the way classes generate a "model of character," in terms of which action-guiding norms of behaviour are to be understood (see 63–78). Przeworski conceives of classes subjectively, Miller objectively.

3. Milton Fisk weds such an objectivist view to a class-based, relativistic ethical theory in his *Ethics and Society* (Brighton: Harvester Press, 1980).

4. Raymond Firth's core definition of a community as "a body of people sharing

common activities and bound by multiple relationships in such a way that the aims of any individual can be achieved only by participation in action with others" is supplemented by the rider that community members "normally" occupy a common territory. Firth adds that communities must include as "constituents essential to social existence" social alignment, social control, social media, and social standards. *Elements of Social Organization* (Boston: Beacon Press, 1963), 41–43. To the "most basic" characteristic of a community, that its members share values in common, Michael Taylor adds that the members must share many values unmediated by formal codes and in such a way that their everyday interactions are altruistic (even if in the long term they expect reciprocity), *Community, Anarchy & Liberty* (Cambridge: Cambridge University Press, 1982), 25–33.

Even though Firth is addressing small communities, his latter three constituents can be brought into phase with the definition employed in this essay if they are regarded as aspects of the way that shared community norms ought to be implicated in ongoing daily life. Taylor's notion of altruism is probably implicated in the idea that shared values are not instrumental. The notion of sharing many values in an unmediated way makes Taylor's definition stronger than the one used here, though he allows that this characteristic is a matter of degree.

5. Alasdair MacIntyre, *After Virtue: A Study in Moral Theory* (Notre Dame, IN: University of Notre Dame Press, 1981), 204–5.

6. Michael Walzer, *Spheres of Justice: A Defense of Pluralism and Equality* (New York: Basic Books, 1983), xiv; for examples of conventionalist views see 28–30, 88n, 134. A pertinent critique is in Joshua Cohen's review of this book in *The Journal of Philosophy*, Vol. 83, No. 8 (August 1986), 457–68.

7. See, e.g., Michael Sandel, *Liberalism and the Limits of Justice* (Cambridge: Cambridge University Press, 1983), 122ff.

8. MacIntyre, *After Virtue*, chap. 15.

9. Charles Taylor, *Hegel*, 377–78, 384. Taylor's more recent *Sources of the Self: The Making of the Modern Identity* (Cambridge, MA: Harvard University Press, 1989), grounds his left communitarian views in a general theory of human nature.

10. Alasdair MacIntyre, *Whose Justice? Which Rationality?* (Notre Dame, IN: University of Notre Dame Press, 1988), 367.

11. Walzer, *Spheres of Justice*, 18, and see his "Philosophy and Democracy," in John S. Nelson, ed., *What Should Philosophy Be Now?* (Albany: State University of New York Press, 1983), 75–99.

12. A democratic-socialist critique/interpretation of Marx's comment is in my "Community, Tradition and the 6th Thesis on Feuerbach," in Kai Nielsen and Robert Ware, eds., *Analysing Marxism* (Calgary: Canadian Journal of Philosophy, Suppl. Vol. 15, 1989), 205–30, some arguments of which are incorporated into this essay.

13. A representative example is the critique by Judy Fudge, "Community or Class: Political Communitarians and Workers' Democracy," in Allan Hutchinson and Leslie Green, eds., *Law and the Community* (Toronto: Carswell, 1989), 57–92.

14. Amy Gutman, "Communitarian Critics of Liberalism," *Philosophy and Public Affairs*, Vol. 14, No. 3 (Summer 1985), 308–22, at 316.

15. Will Kymlicka, "Liberalism and Communitarianism," *Canadian Journal of Philosophy*, Vol. 18, No. 2 (June 1988), 181–203. Kymlicka develops this critique in his

Liberalism, Community, and Culture (Oxford: Clarendon Press, 1989), where he defends such claims as: "We can and should acquire our tasks through freely made personal judgments about the cultural structure, the matrix of understandings and alternatives passed down to us by previous generations, which offer us possibilities we can either affirm or reject" (50–51).

16. MacIntyre, *Whose Justice?* 361–62.
17. *Ibid.*, 387–88.
18. Michael Walzer, *The Company of Critics: Social Criticism and Political Commitment in the 20th Century* (New York: Basic Books, 1988). The supposed ground of possibility for internal critique in Walzer's approach seems to be that of MacIntyre's regarding progress, see 19.
19. Michael Oakeshott, "Political Education," in Michael Sandel, ed., *Liberalism and Its Critics* (New York: New York University Press, 1984), 129–238, at 229.
20. Frederick Engels, "Speech on the 17th Anniversary of the Polish Uprising of 1830," in *Karl Marx, Frederick Engels Collected Works*, Vol. 6 (New York: International Publishers, 1976), 389–90. The speech was made on November 29, 1847.
21. An example is Robert Paul Wolff, *The Poverty of Liberalism* (Boston: Beacon Press, 1968), 192–93.
22. Chapter 3 of *Democratic Theory and Socialism* explicates and defends this conception of democracy.
23. John Dewey, *The Public and Its Problems* (Denver, CO: Alan Swallow, 1957), see, for example, 148.
24. Chapter 4 of *Democratic Theory and Socialism* argues this case.
25. An account of this case is by Anne Bayefsky, "The Human Rights Committee and the Case of Sandra Lovelace," *Canadian Year Book of International Law* (1982), 244.
26. The history of the Japanese-Canadian community and an account of its successful campaign for redress is in Maryka Omatsu, *Bittersweet Passage: Redress and the Japanese Canadian Experience* (Toronto: Between the Lines, 1992).
27. If, following the suggestion of John Rawls regarding theories of justice, one maintains that all normative philosophical theories must be subject to continuing refinement in the light of intuitions which change with changing circumstances and new empirical information, then prescriptions derived from foundational philosophical normative theory must be themselves no more than presumptive. A pertinent treatment of Rawls's method is Norman Daniel's article, "Reflective Equilibrium and Archimedean Points," *Canadian Journal of Philosophy*, Vol. 10, No. 1 (March 1980), 81–103. This topic is more thoroughly covered in Essay 5 of the present collection.
28. The approach is probably in the same "family" as the attempt by Iris Marion Young and others to maintain a "public space" in the face of narrowly exclusionary conceptions of the public and the private on the part of both liberal democrats and civic republicans, and the effort by Drucilla Cornell to defend what she calls "dialogic communitarianism." See Iris Marion Young, "Impartiality and the Civic Public," in Seyla Benhabib and Drucilla Cornell, eds., *Feminism as Critique* (Minneapolis: University of Minnesota Press, 1987), 57–76; Drucilla Cornell, "Beyond Tragedy and Complacency," *Northwestern University Law Review*, Vol. 81, No. 4 (1987), 693–717; and the effort to appropriate Cornell's views from a more individualistic direction by Donna Greschner, "Feminist Concerns with the New

Communitarians," in Hutchinson and Green, eds., *Law and the Community*, 119–50. On the approach of this paper, Young's project is to be seen as a way of conceiving of politics so as to facilitate critique, while Cornell describes one epistemological and social-ontological perspective compatible with such projects.

29. Thus Michael Sandel's appeal to Hannah Arendt, in the "Introduction" to his collection, *Liberalism and Its Critics* (New York: New York University Press, 1984), 7, and Allen Buchanan's response, "Assessing the Communitarian Critique of Liberalism," *Ethics*, Vol. 99, No. 4 (July 1989), 852–82, at 858.

ESSAY 7

Radical Philosophy and the New Social Movements

We all know how many ways philosophers, radical or otherwise, can think of to disagree. Sometimes the disagreements are too trivial for anything but make-work projects, sometimes they are too profound to be nontrivial (who really loses sleep over the question of whether everything is an appearance?), and they often involve theorists from different traditions talking past one another. Exceptions are when those who share common macrovalues disagree in evaluating a living phenomenon over which nonphilosophers also disagree. Such is the case regarding evaluations of the new social movements on the parts, respectively, of Barbara Epstein and of Ernesto Laclau and Chantal Mouffe:

> Through the late eighties radical movements have become increasingly diffuse and divided from one another. Many activists try to comfort themselves by arguing that there is a lot going on on the left; many projects, many organizations. But the fact remains that this activity is not very visible, even to the left itself. The right is in power and has succeeded not only in setting the terms of public discussion but also in winning broad public support. The left has not been able to put forward any effective challenge.[1]

This paper was first published in Roger Gottlieb, ed., *Tradition, Counter-Tradition, Politics* (Philadelphia: Temple University Press, 1993), 199–220. A version was read in a session of the Radical Association at the 1988 Socialist Scholars' Conference, New York. I am grateful to Susan Golding and Roger Gottlieb for helpful comments.

115

We are living [in] . . . one of the most exhilarating moments of the twentieth century: a moment in which new generations, without the prejudices of the past, without theories presenting themselves as "absolute truths" of History, are constructing new emancipatory discourses, more human, diversified and democratic.[2]

The objects of these evaluations are the new social movements—women's, peace, ecological, municipal, antiracist, gay and lesbian, and so on—which in the 1980s and 1990s have increasingly become the focus of attention for socialist and other radical theorists and which have also come to be important players in local and sometimes national and transnational politics.

THEORIZING ABOUT THE NEW SOCIAL MOVEMENTS

From the perspective of socialist vanguard party politics, such movements are regarded as "spontaneous" expressions of popular discontent worthy of attention if they can be made to serve the aims of revolutionary politics claimed to advance the objective interests of the working class. More recent attention to the new social movements, however, rejects any approach that diminishes their importance in terms either of their goals or of their potential as crucial players in a radical transformation of society. Current debates concern the related questions of whether or how the aims of social movements should be prioritized and how, if at all, their activities might be coordinated.

At a limit approaching vanguardism, there is the opinion of Leo Panitch and Ralph Miliband that:

> these movements have undoubtedly enlarged and enriched the meaning of socialism. All such movements are an essential part of the coalition of forces on which a socialist movement must depend. However, no such "new social movement" can obviate the need for a socialist party (or parties). Nor can they replace organized labour as the main force on which a socialist movement must rely.[3]

At another limit is the sort of position expressed by Gavin Kitching:

> Left activity should . . . not be directed to "making socialists" at all. For if this is not something that can be done within the conventional parameters of politics then a Left political activity should not be about "creating socialists" but about involving people in specific struggles around specific issues.[4]

Between these positions are those that call for some sort of association—a "democratic alliance" as Joshua Cohen and Joel Rogers call it[5]—which is more than a series of *ad hoc* coalitions but less than a political party. Among many other discussions of this topic are those of Sheila Rowbotham and the other authors of the influential *Beyond the Fragments*, Samuel Bowles and Herbert Gintis, Jean Cohen, Stanley Aronowitz, and Laclau and Mouffe.[6] With the important exceptions of Claus Offe and Rudolph Bahro, who make reference to the Green Party, and of Sheila Collins, in her defence of the Rainbow Coalition's relation to the Democratic Party,[7] the forms such associations might take are left unspecified.

One reason for this is that we now have a generation of radicals who have experienced the shortcomings both of organized left-wing party politics and of such things as the student and antiwar movements in efforts toward a social transformation (indeed, who often find themselves confronting neo-liberal political hegemony instead) and who are accordingly cautious about making organizational prescriptions. Another source of indecision, however, is that there are disagreements with theoretical implications.

For example, while Aronowitz seeks ways to ascertain how one social movement may come to acquire the "moral authority" enabling it "to set the agenda for left politics," Cohen and Rogers insist that an alliance be built around a "democratic principle" which precludes such a privileged role.[8] These are not the sorts of disagreements that can be resolved by appeal to conditions for organizational effectiveness, since they involve contested theoretical claims. Thus, it is neither surprising nor inappropriate that a good deal of debate pertaining to the new social movements has been highly theoretical in nature. Nonetheless, it seems to me that the main arguments are still too abstract.

Some contributions to the debate ought to be set aside, since despite their colourful prose, they are easily seen to be pejoratively ideological in rushing to conclusions by grossly misrepresenting positions they contest or by advancing transparently unsound arguments. An example of the first tendency is the sweeping attack by Ellen Meiksins Wood on nearly all the left champions of new social movements, when she incorrectly attributes to them the view that social transformation will come about through "a nonantagonistic process of institutional reform" led by intellectuals and motivated by "a disembodied democratic impulse."[9]

An example of the second sort of dead end is Perry Anderson's prioritization of working-class struggle over women's liberation on the ground that the latter is essentially individualistic, being rooted in "the division of labour between the sexes," which is "a fact of nature: it cannot be abolished, as can the division between classes, a fact of history."[10] How could Anderson have failed to acquire at least second-hand knowledge of the mountain of feminist literature attacking such an identification of sex and gender?

To be distinguished from these sorts of intervention are attempts to construct a theory, or a metatheory, of society by reference to which social movements may be situated. One example is the concept of "social positions" sketched by Bowles and Gintis in which power is "heterogeneous," and another is the social ontology explicated by Laclau and Mouffe based on the inescapable "nonfixity" of "social positions."[11] Or, arguing from the side of prescribed working-class prioritization, there is Milton Fisk's distinction between a society's "basic framework," which is an economic structure, and its "stimulus causes," which may be any of a number of extraclass oppressions or struggles against oppression.[12] Reflection on these attempts usefully structures thought about social movements and their possible relations to radical social transformation; and the debates they have sparked, such as those between Laclau/Mouffe and Norman Geras[13] and between Fisk and his critics,[14] illustrate how deep the philosophical roots of these political disputes go.

However, after initial exchanges, the debates take on a "stuck record" character, the form of which is familiar to any student of the history of philosophy. Positions get staked out with reference to some live question (for example, about the relation of science to religion in the case of medieval debates over nominalism and realism or about determinism in history with respect to controversies over laws and explanation in nineteenth-century German and again in twentieth-century Anglo-Saxon philosophy of history). Heated debate soon loses all but perfunctory reference to its originating questions. And warring camps, rallying around heroes and attacking villains, find alternative language in which to repeat abstract charges and counter-charges. In the case of debates over new social movements, positions are reiterated over whether the working class should be taken as primary in strategies for radical social change and whether such strategizing can or should be grounded in foundational theory of social philosophy.

Now what would count as an appropriate answer to such questions depends in part on how key terms—notably "primary" or "foundational"—are meant, but even an answer that makes sense can fail to respond to questions that need answering. As a first step toward formulating questions and hypothesizing at least directions for response to them, I prescribe that radical philosophers enter the terrain of actual politics. By this I do not mean just that radical philosophers should, according to the accepted formula, preface statements of their theories with admonitions to make philosophy relevant to struggle and conclude with comments about political strategy, but that they should engage in what might be called, with reference to the topic of this essay, the "critical interrogation" of social movements. Since consistency requires that the essay itself engage in such critical interrogation in a way that is atypical of philosophical essays (radical or otherwise), perhaps I shall be forgiven for indulging in a bit of autobiography to introduce this concept.

In thinking through the topics addressed in *Democratic Theory and Socialism*, I found that at nearly every crucial point, "data" available only through internal critiques of movement politics were required in order to make theoretical advances. Accordingly, I prescribed that democratic-socialist researchers undertake this activity,[15] hoping readers would not notice the nearly complete absence of such concrete inquiry in the very work prescribing it and that others would undertake the called-for studies. The gap was noticed, however, and I was not to escape my own prescription. The reason for this was that the Canadian Society for Socialist Studies had undertaken to publish its 1988 annual on the theme of new social movements,[16] and I was hardly in a position to avoid doing editorial work on the project. Nor do I regret doing the work.

We sent letters to a large number of radicals who were active in social movements in Canada asking them to share with our readers something of the history of their movements and to reflect on their strengths and weaknesses as potential players in a radical social transformation. The result was a mixed bag of contributions by those who had time to write something and with different relative emphases on descriptive accounts and prescriptions. We found that we could sort out those parts of an account that were rooted in actual experience from those deduced from radical theories some authors brought with them to the project; and, thanks to direct acquaintance with some of the movements, we knew that alternative, sometimes strongly conflicting, accounts were possible. Still, the range of movements represented was broad: Parent Power in Toronto, a standing International Women's Day committee, defence of abortion clinics, an organization of visible minority women, a coalition of peace movements, gays against the police, a coalition of trade unions in Quebec, an organization of disabled women, a labour-ecology alliance, and others.

Reading the critical accounts was most enlightening. Putting aside (as far as one can) ideas already formed about how social movements might relate to radical change, we read and reread the contributions, trying to draw conclusions rooted in the authors' own critical reflections. We concluded that the fruit of much more such interrogation is required on the part of radical theorists addressing the new social movements. Indeed, if I am not mistaken, the most important radical theorizing to date has been carried on in just this way, namely, in critical reflection by socialists on trade-union and other working-class movements and by feminists on movements of women. More specifically, common characteristics of otherwise quite diverse movements challenge some socialist-theoretical preconceptions about the new social movements and suggest ways that philosophers might participate in projects of radical transformation.

NEW SOCIAL MOVEMENTS: SOME CHARACTERISTICS

Some features of the movements discussed in the Socialist Studies publication are well known to movement activists, old and new. Chief among these are the money problem, the problem of developing leadership, the problem of momentum, and the problem of burnout. The authors seem to place a high priority on ensuring that however leadership is developed and exercised, it not be carried out at the expense of organization democracy, and one senses a less moralistic, more sympathetic approach to the inevitable toll of burnout on a movement's members.

More interesting for the purpose at hand than these problems are two features often misrepresented in left-wing conceptions: that movement participants are content to operate within the boundaries of existing states while shunning either revolutionary or reformist political party activity, and that these movements are single-issue associations. Neither characterization is adequate to the ways the activists we listened to regard their efforts, and at least the second supposes a paradigm inappropriate to conceptualizing the new social movements or a project of radical social transformation to which they might contribute.

The State and the Parties

Contrary to the notion of social movements as content to manoeuvre within present states, we found general scepticism about the state reported by authors in the collection. Sometimes this is reflected in central debates over directions carried on within a movement, such as is reported by Susan Prentice, when she discusses the controversy between those who wanted the main emphasis of the day care movement in which she is involved to be on community-run, local day care and those who wanted state-run day care.[17] Even those in the latter camp, however, recognized that democratic control of the quality of state-run day care and continuing community input are essential, and they shared with members of other movements a realization that all levels of the state in Canada work much more against accessible, quality day care than for it. Thus, at the same time that they were concerned to pressure appropriate state bodies to make gains, movement activists almost never saw this as the only goal, and achievements were always conjoined with appreciation that such gains are precarious.

A more accurate way of regarding the relation of new social movements to the state than that of simply asking how far they pursue goals through it is Offe's approach. The collection in which his essay on the topic appears is dedicated to examining "the changing boundaries of the political" occasioned by the growth of the new social movements. Offe characterizes something as "political" when it is considered an appropriate candidate to be a matter of binding public policy (arrived at by generally recognized means). His claim is that the new social movements have sometimes succeeded in forcing what had been merely private concerns into forums of public debate over whether they should be political concerns and sometimes in making them political in this sense.[18] Thus regarded, the new social movements are engaged in a far more radical enterprise than the caricature suggests — namely, challenging the contours of the public and the private.

Similar comments apply to the stance of the social movements toward political parties. Here again, it would be wrong to classify them as either anti- or proparty. One reason members of social movements resist subsumption in party politics is that the shifting of alliances is seen as making this difficult. A more general worry has to do with a bias for participatory democracy built into movement politics: After all, the belief that direct action by voluntary movements of people is possible and desirable contributes to their joining social movements. The general scepticism about political parties is that they will insist on mediating between movement aims and action. At the same time, just as the state is recognized simultaneously as an obstacle and as a locus of potential gain, so are parties, or at least parties that have some claim to being on the left.

This is quite evident in the case of Canada's social-democratic, New Democratic Party (NDP), which employs explicitly socialist rhetoric (sometimes) and has a certain base in organized labour. Those authors who discuss this party pragmatically regard it as a presence, like the state, to be profited from or to be gotten around, depending on the circumstances. Moreover, rather than being either for or against the NDP, all contributors, including those who are members of it, perceive both the potentialities and limits of this party, and often express the view that important gains can be made by and through it, provided that movements maintain a certain distance. Collins reflects a similar stance regarding the Vermont Rainbow Coalition's relation to the Democratic Party.[19]

Single Issues

The main caricature I wish to address is that new social movements are objectionably single issued. In one respect, any movement clearly does direct its attention to a single cluster of issues—namely, those whose oppressive features have motivated people to form and join the movement. On a traditional socialist view, this is seen as a severe limitation on the potential of new social movements to effect a radical social transformation. Radical champions of movement politics, on the other hand, see issue orientation not only as an inevitable feature of present-day activism, but also as a healthy precursor to the pluralism they regard as central to a transformed society.[20]

Reflection on the contributions to our volume lends support to the latter perspective by indicating ways that movement politics may simultaneously be rooted in specific concerns while broadening the horizons of their members' aspirations and laying the basis for conjoined activities. Of course, on a traditional socialist perspective, this is just what is supposed to happen (and sometimes has happened) in the case of working-class movements. Critical interrogation of social movements reveals how this can take place without having to posit a dubious historical metaphysics within which one group's aims are supposed somehow to embody those of all the rest.

The topic can be addressed first by considering some cultural dimensions of movement politics as perceived by activists themselves. I suppose it is a commonplace that political movement activity has as one of its effects partially to "construct" the identities of participants and that in the course of movement politics symbols play an important role both internal to a movement and in defining the movement to those outside of it. What is striking about the contributions to the volume is the number of activists who are conscious of these dimensions of movement politics and who place them at the centre of their concerns in what might be called a "noninstrumental" way. That is, while many political activists have regarded forging an identity of members with a movement as a way to maintain loyalty, authors in our survey who treat the subject perceive, rather, that a principal aim of the movement is to create a sense of pride and self-worth.

Thus, Joanne Doucette and Sharon Stone of the Disabled Women's Network see their movement's struggles as victorious even when specific political aims were not achieved, since the spectacle of disabled women assertively defending themselves broke the helpless, "wheelchair" image of the disabled both to the world and to the disabled women themselves. Carmencita Hernandez cites the ability of visible minority women to secure a speaker's place at a mainstream women's conference as a major victory: "When [our speaker] Fely Villasin mounted the stage it was a statement made by the [visible minority] women: We can speak for ourselves!"[21] Although from the point of view of securing some specific political goal aimed at by the conference, this was no doubt an event of slight moment, it helped to play an important role in the project of identity construction. This is one way that the movement exceeded single issuism.

Also in a noninstrumental way, activities of a movement, even a movement itself, come to take on symbolic significance beyond themselves (the "signifier comes to exceed the signified," as Laclau somewhere put it in making a similar point). Thus, Patricia Antonyshyn and others report how an escort service to help women run a gauntlet of intimidating protesters, initially in defence of Toronto's Henry Morgenthaler abortion clinic, became symbolic of the struggle for women's emancipation generally. And Tim McCaskell notes the way that a Right to Privacy Committee, formed for the specific purpose of defending those rounded up in a massive police raid against the gay baths, "*was* the gay community" of Toronto and beyond.[22] These examples are noninstrumental partly in virtue of the fact that nobody in the movement set out to "create" a symbolic event or organization.

At the same time, it is misleading to regard movement-embodied symbols functionally, as Offe does in explaining their role as "[making] up for lack of formal organization."[23] Movement activists seem well aware of the potential of any of their actions (slogans, names, high-profile members, etc.) to take on symbolic significance, and they welcome this, not for the sake of internal cohesion, but for the sake of the aims of the movement. This point is of more than obvious significance, as is seen in trying to explicate the phrase "aims of the movement." The symbols movements create simultaneously are occasioned by and extend beyond the immediate issues that generate them. We shall return to this point after noting some additional features of social movements that strain a paradigm wherein social movements are contrasted with revolutionary political parties. Such a contrast is no doubt appropriate to the extent that it is thought essential to revolutionary parties that they act in accord with a well-defined and comprehensive plan (from which "correct lines" can be derived on any topic).

However, I suspect that those with this notion of a nonsingle-issue organization in mind think of the new social movements as interest groups of the sort the 1950s political-scientific pluralists liked to study; but there are significant differences. Unlike interest groups, movement aims are expected by participants to *expand* to the extent that the movement is a healthy one. Prentice develops this topic in her account of the day care campaign, tracing the history whereby the button slogan "Universal Care" came to be replaced by "Kids Are Not for Profit," and McCaskell explicates the process of internal questioning about the motives for the bath-house raids which led participants in the movement to expand its aims from defence of those charged by the police to a more general attack on police power and the structure of municipal decision making. Similarly, Kari Dehli and the others discussing a local effort by parents to secure some control over the quality of education in their children's school address the way this led to a broader campaign concerned with teacher training, heritage language, and the political economy of municipal education policy.[24]

Yet another difference between social movements (at least those of our survey) and interest groups is that virtually all of their participants saw the forming of alliances with others as not only advantageous, but as a good thing in itself, and nearly all the authors describe concerted efforts to seek more or less stable liaison with other movements. No doubt this can be explained in part after the manner of Hilary Wainwright by reference to the interconnectedness of capitalist, state, and patriarchal sources of oppression and by Offe's explanation in terms of the need of weak movements to draw on one another's strength,[25] but these explanations do not get to the heart of the matter. Rather than looking at general causes for the forming of alliances, it seems more fruitful to attend to some aspects of movement politics that make alliances possible. I shall discuss two such aspects, one relating to what is called "the paradox of success" by Antonyshyn, *et al.* and another in relation to shared visions.

The Paradox of Success

The term "paradox of success" is used to indicate the problem for a movement that to the extent it succeeds in gaining whatever goal motivated its formation, it loses membership and momentum. This problem is considered more grave by some of the authors than by others, and I speculate that how grave it is seen to be depends on whether one harbours the goal of an umbrella political party and hopes that a specific movement can be turned into one. It is certainly true that insofar as they are oriented to a specific range of goals, social movements are greatly impeded from turning into such parties; however, this is also one of their strengths from the point of view of forming alliances, since it simultaneously makes them nonthreatening and defines a range of issues on which joint action can be taken. Laurie Adkin's and Catherine Alpaugh's description of the labour/ecology alliance in Windsor-Detroit, The People for Clean Air Alliance, is typical:

> Backgrounds and interests are varied, and the coalition has already experienced serious divisions. Its members are determined, however, to tolerate these differences and to coalesce around the goal of stopping the [Detroit] incinerator.[26]

It follows from this account of having limited goals as a relative strength that an alliance is threatened by the "danger" of success (to date, alas, this danger is still remote in Windsor and Detroit), just as it is by the heterogeneity of its membership. But as Alpaugh and Adkin explain, the compensating feature of the alliance is that it has helped to nurture an alternate vision of society on the part of its members.

> For many of those who have taken a stand against the city government and their corporate partners, it has illuminated a whole new way of looking at society. It's not just the incinerator that has to be stopped, but this insane world of "unlimited" production and consumption. An industrially produced environmental crisis is here, and only a direct confrontation with industrial society and its power structure will turn it around. What we need . . . is a vision of a different way of life based on *being* not on *having*.[27]

To the extent that participation in a coalition is one of the things that generates such a vision, this makes the paradox of success itself paradoxical, or rather, dialectical. Having relatively limited goals helps to facilitate alliances, which in turn expands participants' goals.

Visions

Consideration of the notion of visions takes us back to the way movements embody symbols. Most radical philosophers of my generation recall how specific movements against the war in Vietnam came to be thought of first as parts of *the* antiwar movement (even though there never was a centrally coordinated movement) and then as a symbol of human emancipation generally. In this case (and perhaps also in the evolution of the women's movement), the expansion of symbolic significance and the development of a vision drove each other, but one might say that symbolic expansion was the leading force: The vision as a widespread phenomenon gelled in response to the symbol. In the new social movements it strikes me that the vision is rather more up front from the beginning; that is, visions partly motivate the conscious creation and expansion of symbols.[28] Moreover, contrary to what critics of social-movement-oriented politics such as Wood allege,[29] there are some fairly clear convergences among visions reported, and they are more specific than just "humanism." In particular, anticapitalist, antistatist, and prodemocratic values are common features of each movement's visions. Most include an antipatriarchal value, and many include antiracist values as well.

RADICAL PHILOSOPHY IN MOVEMENT POLITICS

An important task of philosophers in the first category is to contribute to the understanding and advancement of the cultural dimensions of movement activity discussed above. So far this has largely fallen to promovement theorists with training in literary disciplines. The growing interest in discourse and poststructuralist theory in North American philosophy is beginning to bring radical philosophers into this area of work to the extent that sometimes controversies over the importance of the new social movements proceed as if this were essentially a debate about the merits of discourse theory itself.

But viewed as political projects of creating symbol-driven projects to affect political consciousness and action on the part of movement activists, useful contributions can be made by philosophers from a variety of other orientations, addressing questions, for example, of personal identity, language, or the phenomenology of self and other. There is also room to question traditionally assumed boundaries among cultural analysis, political theory, and economics, which philosophers, again from different traditions, adept at classifying "the disciplines," might challenge.

In the adjunct category there are several additional, fairly obvious tasks. (a) Understanding the political economy of a society in respect to the problems and possibilities faced by new social movements requires the work of philosophers as well as theorists trained in economics, for example, to address questions of economic determination or ways of conceiving macroeconomic orders, such as capitalism or socialism.[30] (b) Participants in movements against racist, sexist, national, and other oppressions need to continue pursuing thought about the historical and sustaining origins of these oppressions, about which all the easy answers have already been given. (c) The ecology movement has put several concepts usefully on the agenda, some of which—"sustainability," "empowerment," "transgenerational obligation," and others—need theoretical elaboration. (d) Insofar as movements politically campaign to gain and defend group rights, this concept and the related ontological question of the relation of groups to individuals require ongoing work. Many more examples come to mind.

A point of entry to the question of what (relatively) unique philosophical work remains is to consider the difficulty of ascertaining criteria for what counts as a movement enjoying "successes." In his contribution to the Socialist Studies Annual, David Langille sets down criteria—effecting major changes in public policy, achieving the stated goals of a movement, changing public opinion, laying the ground for continuing effectiveness, and changing the structure of society as a whole[31]—but there are too many of them, and they require interpretation. Offe cites the simple criterion of succeeding in making an issue a matter of public policy debate,[32] but this seems to leave too much out. A task for philosophers, then, is to figure out what "movement success" might mean and how to go about ascertaining when or to what degree it is achieved (or even whether it is desirable to try ascertaining this). One reason I think this is both a useful and a uniquely philosophical task is that it brings one up against theory-laden issues with practical implications about which there is ongoing debate on the part of movement activists: to whit, reform, revolution, and unity of vision.

Reform and Revolution

In thinking about traditional ways of making the reform-revolution distinction (revolution as discontinuous with the past, reform as continuous; revolution as extra-electoral, reform as electoral; and so on), it is not too difficult to carry out the destructive job of showing inadequacies of this paradigm.[33] More difficult is to develop a theory of social transformation that would yield categories appropriate for conceptualizing political activity not now well described (or well carried out) as either revolutionary or reformist.

A hypothesis to focus radical philosophical tasks in this regard comes to mind when we reflect on the most general feature of all social movement goals (central to the more limited task of defining "socialism" in Essays 3 and 4, above, and clearly recognized by all movement participants) to overcome systemic oppression. The hypothesis is that in place of a classification of movements, policies, or activities into those that are revolutionary in one of this word's traditional left-wing senses and those that are reformist, such things should be designated "radical" (or "transformatory" or, indeed, "revolutionary"—as nothing is meant to hinge on the terminology) when they are likely to make antioppressive progress. To my way of thinking, this means that they must actually attack at least some of whatever makes a specifically resisted oppression systemic (for example, sexist or racist educational institutions and not just individual prejudicial attitudes) *and* that relative success in resistance to one form of oppression must not be purchased by inhibiting antioppressive progress with respect to other forms of oppression.

This seems to me enough to characterize radical politics. On this perspective, the line between radical and nonradical politics is not sharp, and such questions as what sorts of activities can make the most progress in specific circumstances or when nonradical politics is to be encouraged (or allowed, or resisted) are matters of political judgment that take account of local circumstances. In keeping with the second criterion of radicalness, radical politics will always involve trying to find ways to make movement activities mutually reinforcing and to avoid advancing one movement at the expense of others. Sometimes "necessary evil" types of choices must be made that involve ranking two or more movement activities as to importance. For reasons given elsewhere, I believe that even admitting the possibility of such lamentable situations, such estimations should be made on a case-by-case basis and that it is a mistake for radical philosophers to seek criteria for a general ranking.[34]

Let me be clear about the focus of this prescription. It is not denied that radicals should seek out sources of oppression, as this is clearly required to identify their systemic natures. Nor should radicals be inattentive to the interrelation of different forms of oppression. The worry some seem to have that absence of a shared macrotheory of history and society will lead to mutually isolating attitudes is belied by the critical interrogation of actual movement politics. Among the movement activists of our study were some with different general theoretical orientations (Marxist, non-Marxist feminist, deep ecological, and so on) and some who seemed contentedly agnostic about macrotheoretical controversy. None had any trouble seeing how such things as class, race, or sex oppression reinforce one another, and it is fair to conclude that each of them was receptive to making use of theoretically guided empirical and political analysis carried on from within any orientation, provided it was practically helpful in understanding such things.

It is not even being claimed that seeking to discover a "direction" to history or proving something to be the ultimate and sole source of all oppression is *necessarily* doomed to failure. That is, a prescription against making this the prime or definitive pursuit of the radical philosopher is not deductively based on a theory of knowledge, language, or human nature. (Although, as we see at the end of this essay, room also remains for traditional philosophical work, carried on by philosophers who may be radicals.) The prescription is derived, rather, from critical interrogation of the history of movement politics, within which claims to philosophically based privilege for one movement have worked *against* such politics. What is being insisted on is that radical philosophers embed their labour within movement politics in focusing on the problematic questions they address and in evaluating alternative solutions. This applies, also, to radical philosophers who persist in seeking ultimate foundations of oppression or primary struggles. I suspect that critical movement interrogation would force such a person profoundly to rethink such questions as what constitutes "primacy" or "a foundation."

By contrast, continued consideration of the notion of oppression and of the topic just set aside of unity of vision suggests some questions appropriately addressed by philosophers that go somewhat beyond adjunct work. The claim of this paper that such questions can be addressed adequately— that is, in such a way as to advance radical politics—without reference to macrophilosophical theory cannot be refuted without circularity or triviality by appeal to macrophilosophical principles, but then it also cannot be supported without actually trying, which is what the essay prescribes.

One question concerns "systematicity." I have the impression that movement activists have insufficiently precise concepts of what makes some form of discrimination systematic and that those radical philosophers who have addressed this subject typically argue backward, that is, to justify an antecedent conviction that, for example, capitalism or patriarchy is primarily oppressive. A constructive use of philosophical talents might, then, be to address the concept of what makes an oppression systemic (or systematic or structural).

Another task pertains to the term "oppression" itself. I do not see how this or any analogous term can be voided of normative implications. It is not just that the aspirations of some category of people are generally thwarted that makes them suffer oppression, but that in addition this is morally unjustifiable. I am not suggesting that radical philosophers function as moralists or that they try to persuade movement activists to accept a favoured ethical theory. Rather, I believe that the approach to moral questions evolved in "applied ethics," where philosophers closely reflect on actual social or institutional situations to help organize thought by drawing out moral implications and sorting types of reasons and relevant considerations, be brought to bear on topics pertinent to social movement activism.[35]

Visions Again

Radical philosophizing that focuses on oppression necessarily has a negative orientation, since the dimension of "movement success" it is designed to facilitate is combative. Debates over unity of vision have a positive focus. Thus Collins states:

> It was precisely a coherent moral vision that was missing from the populist, single issue, and community-organizing politics of so many white activists during the 1970s. . . . The revival of ethical and moral values in the arena of national policy was perhaps the true genius of the Jackson campaign of 1984. The ability to gain wider adherence to these values and to translate them into specific policy proposals and political strategies will be the real litmus test of the Rainbow Coalition's viability.[36]

This point of view at once challenges that of Kitching, quoted near the beginning of the essay, which denies that unity of vision is required at all, and that perspective which insists that unity of view must be anchored in goals specific to one hegemonic movement.

If, with Collins, one rejects these alternatives, there remains the problem of finding a normative basis for shared values that is at once universally motivating and compatible with the pluralism required for any politics carried on jointly by movements with different goals: to construct a concept of democracy that helps one to achieve unity in difference. It is recognition of this problem that leads Laclau and Mouffe to reject what they see as an objectionably foundationist and antipluralist essentialism. This, in turn, has prompted the reply (for example, of Geras)[37] that in rejecting what they call essentialism, Laclau and Mouffe lose any possible grounding for unity of action.

I think the reply to Geras by Laclau and Mouffe on this score is on the right track:

> By locating socialism in the wider field of the democratic revolution, we have indicated that the political transformations which will eventually enable us to transcend capitalist society are founded on the plurality of social agents and of their struggles. Thus the field of social conflict is extended, rather than being concentrated in a "privileged agent" of social change. This also means that the extension and radicalization of democratic struggles does not have a final point of arrival in the achievement of a fully liberated society.[38]

Of more interest to the task now at hand than the debates in which Mouffe and Laclau have been involved, over nonfoundationism and working-class primacy, is that aspect of their efforts addressing a difficult problem they share with the many other radical theorists who similarly highlight democracy. This is to defend the normative value of democracy as a unifying vision and at the same time to avoid making it a supervalue that overrides particular movement-specific ones, thus in a paradoxical way democratically undercutting democratic pluralism.

The task is problematic because there is a temptation for philosophers to make apodictic prescription, and in the case of those philosophers who support radical movement politics (even those who reject foundationism) this will be compounded by movement fragility. As all the authors of our study noted, sustaining new or old social movements is difficult, in part because of the heterogeneity of goals among movements and in part because of the heterogeneity of values among the members of a single movement (aside from the shared antioppressive values that brought them together). Thus, there is an impetus for movement radicals to seek overarching values as a kind of glue. Movement-friendly radical philosophers, then, rally to the call and do what we are best trained to do (produce general philosophical theories) in order to justify democracy as the sought-after common value.

Closer examination of movement heterogeneity helps to show how the temptation in question might be countered. From our survey of social movements, I concluded that participants considered the problem of *inter*movement heterogeneity more grave than the problem of *intra*movement heterogeneity.[39] The reason for this is that the former challenges much-needed coalitions, while the latter becomes threatening as a movement begins to confront the "paradox of success." When an oppressive force is still strong, it serves as a common enemy uniting members of a movement with otherwise divergent values. This means that there is an inverse relation between the gravity of the heterogeneity problem in actual politics and the difficulty of philosophically defending pluralist democracy.

Intermovement cooperation can be pragmatically defended by appeal to the common advantages of democratic forums for reaching consensus or negotiating differences and of promoting intermovement pluralistic mutual respect for maintaining coalition solidarity. To the extent that philosophical skills are required at all in this regard, they are interior to intermovement democratic politics (for example, to help activists find common ground by distinguishing avoidable and unavoidable conflict, real versus apparent difference, and so on). To some extent, intramovement heterogeneity can also be pragmatically addressed, but depending on how radically different are movement members' concepts of such things as what constitutes a good life, pragmatic solutions alone are strained, and they become more so as movements succeed. When oppressive limitations to people leading their lives as they wish are breached, questions about how a meaningful life should or can be led come to the fore.

In these circumstances, radical philosophical work is called for to provide conceptual frameworks to reconcile specifically democratic and extra-democratic values. Mouffe's and Laclau's efforts to wed a neo-Gramscian political theory to antifoundationist linguistic theory is one approach. Carol Gould's modified foundationist theory to ground democracy in a concept of individual freedom is another, as is Iris Marion Young's solution in terms of a pluralized theory of justice, and other approaches[40]—whether complementary or not it may be too soon to ascertain—come to mind.

Such philosophical work is the sort that could also be potentially useful when confronting decisions about whether or how appropriate forms of ongoing cross-movement organization might be constructed, since in this case heterogeneity can be anticipated to persist. Here, prescriptions about necessary organizational forms are not deduced by the radical philosopher and dictated to activists; rather, movement-embedded philosophical theories are of potential use to radical movement activists confronting context-specific political questions.

Radical philosophers may also wish to address such questions as what the meaning of life is, and they may even wish to defend the view that democracy, somehow regarded, *is* after all the supreme value. From the perspective of this essay, such efforts are in one respect extrapolitical. The tasks of the radical philosopher *qua* radical[41] are to act as an adjunct to antioppressive politics in the ways suggested above, to employ appropriate philosophical skills to identify systemic oppression, and to help integrate democratic and extrademocratic values in radical political activity. True, the prescribed contribution of the philosopher to this project is less orderly and its conclusions are less decisive than radical philosophizing that deduces a comprehensive position from principles of whatever the philosopher thinks is the font of politics. But does it not seem that if such an approach could have succeeded it already would have done so?

Notes

1. Barbara Epstein, "Rethinking Social Movement Theory," *Socialist Review*, Vol. 20, No. 1 (January/March 1990), 57.
2. Ernesto Laclau and Chantal Mouffe, *Hegemony and Socialist Strategy: Toward a Radical Democratic Politics* (London: Verso, 1985), 80.
3. Ralph Miliband and Leo Panitch, "Socialists and the 'New Conservatism,'" *Socialist Register: 1987* (London: Merlin, 1987), 512–13.
4. Gavin Kitching, "A Reply to Ellen Meiksins Wood," *New Left Review*, No. 163 (May/June 1987), 121–28, at 128.
5. Joshua Cohen and Joel Rogers, *On Democracy: Toward a Transformation of American Society* (Harmondsworth: Penguin, 1983), 173–75.
6. Sheila Rowbotham, Lynne Segal, and Hilary Wainwright, *Beyond the Fragments: Feminism and the Making of Socialism* (Boston: Alyson, 1979); Samuel Bowles and Herbert Gintis, *Democracy and Capitalism* (New York: Basic Books, 1986); Jean L. Cohen, *Class and Civil Society* (Amherst: University of Massachusetts Press,

1982); Stanley Aronowitz, *The Crisis in Historical Materialism* (New York: Praeger, 1981); Laclau and Mouffe, *Hegemony and Socialist Strategy*.

7. Claus Offe, "Challenging the Boundaries of Institutional Politics: Social Movements since the 1960s," in Charles S. Maier, ed., *Changing Boundaries of the Political* (New York: Cambridge University Press, 1987), 63–105; and Claus Offe, *Contradictions of the Welfare State* (Cambridge, MA: MIT Press, 1984). Rudolf Bahro, *From Red to Green* (London: Verso, 1984). Sheila D. Collins, *The Rainbow Challenge: The Jackson Campaign and the Future of U.S. Politics* (New York: Monthly Review Press, 1986).

8. Stanley Aronowitz, "Theory and Socialist Strategy," *Social Text*, No. 16 (Winter 1986–87), 1–16, at 14; Cohen and Rogers, *On Democracy*, 174–75.

9. Ellen Meiksins Wood, *The Retreat from Class* (London: Verso, 1986), see chap. 9.

10. Perry Anderson, *In the Tracks of Historical Materialism* (London: Verso, 1983), 91.

11. Bowles and Gintis, *Democracy*, see 96–98. Laclau and Mouffe, *Hegemony*, chap. 3.

12. Milton Fisk, "Feminism, Socialism, and Historical Materialism," *Praxis International*, Vol. 2, No. 2 (July 1982), 117–40.

13. Norman Geras, "A Critique of Laclau and Mouffe" and "Ex-Marxism without Substance," in *New Left Review*, No. 163 (May/June 1987) and No. 169 (May/June 1989). Ernesto Laclau and Chantal Mouffe, "Post-Marxism without Apologies," *New Left Review*, No. 166 (November/December 1987), 79–106. Despite the fact that the specialized audience interested in the details of this debate will have already read it in the *New Left Review*, Geras has seen fit to reproduce and reiterate his contributions in his *Discourses of Extremity* (London: Verso, 1990), thus spinning the "stuck record" referred to below. By contrast, though surely continuing importantly to differ, Milton Fisk and Ernesto Laclau have turned to more creative work: Fisk, *The State and Justice: An Essay in Political Theory* (Cambridge: Cambridge University Press, 1989); Laclau, *New Reflections on the Revolution of Our Times* (London: Verso, 1990).

14. Milton Fisk, "Why the Anti-Marxists Are Wrong," *Monthly Review*, Vol. 38, No. 10 (March 1987), 7–17, and "A Basis for Solidarity: Reply to Wrabley & Albert," *Monthly Review*, Vol. 39, No. 7 (December 1987), 50–55. Ray Wrabley, "Milton Fisk and the Anti-Marxists," and Michael Albert, "Why Marxism Isn't the Activist's Answer," *Monthly Review*, Vol. 39, No. 7 (December 1987), 41–42 and 43–49, respectively.

15. Frank Cunningham, *Democratic Theory and Socialism* (Cambridge: Cambridge University Press, 1987), 210–11, 229–30.

16. Frank Cunningham, Sue Findlay, Marlene Kadar, Alan Lennon, and Ed Silva, eds., *Social Movements/Social Change*, 1988 volume of *Socialist Studies/Etudes Socialistes* (Toronto: Between the Lines, 1988) (hereafter *Social Movements*). Copies of this volume may be obtained from the publisher, Between the Lines, 394 Euclid Avenue, Toronto, Canada M6G 2S9.

17. Susan Prentice, "'Kids Are Not for Profit': The Politics of Day Care," in *Social Movements*, 98–128.

18. Offe, "Challenging the Boundaries," 71.

19. Collins, *Rainbow Challenge*, 319ff.

20. The point is well developed and argued in Iris Marion Young's *Justice and the*

Politics of Difference (Princeton, NJ: Princeton University Press, 1990), chap. 6.

21. Sharon D. Stone and Joanne Doucette, "Organizing the Marginalized: The Disabled Women's Network, in *Social Movements*, 81–97; Carmencita Hernandez, "Visible Minority Women," in *Social Movements*, 157–68, at 161.

22. Patricia Antonyshyn, B. Lee, and Alex Merrill, "Marching for Women's Lives: The Campaign for Free-Standing Abortion Clinics in Ontario," in *Social Movements*, 129–58; Tim McCaskell, "The Bath Raids and Gay Politics," in *Social Movements*, 169–86, at 172.

23. Offe, "Challenging the Boundaries," 94.

24. Kari Dehli, John Restakis, and Errol Sharpe, "The Rise and Demise of the Parent Movement in Toronto," in *Social Movements*, 209–27.

25. Hilary Wainwright, in Sheila Rowbotham, *et al.*, eds., *Fragments*, 4. Offe, "Challenging the Boundaries," 93–94.

26. Laurie E. Adkin and Catherine Alpaugh, "Labour, Ecology, and the Politics of Convergence," in *Social Movements*, 48–73, at 58.

27. *Ibid.*, 59.

28. This marks a difference from earlier social movements not noted by David Plotke in his criticism of those who see a new "cultural politics" in the new social movements, "What's So New about New Social Movements," *Socialist Review*, Vol. 20, No. 1 (January/March 1990), 81–102, see 89–92. A main thesis of Plotke's argument is that radical champions of the new social movements overestimate their importance because they are preoccupied with rejecting an ossified version of Marxism. It is noteworthy, however, that the activist authors whose reports we studied had very little or nothing at all to say for or against either Marxist or non-Marxist theoretical frameworks.

29. Wood, *Retreat from Class*, 179.

30. Some interesting suggestions along these lines are in Paul Browne, "Reification, Class and 'New Social Movements,'" *Radical Philosophy*, No. 55 (Summer 1990), 18–24. In my view, these suggestions can stand independently of Browne's attempt to show that a Lukácsized Marxism preserves a class-centric approach to new social movements.

31. David Langille, "Building an Effective Peace Movement: One Perspective," in *Social Movements*, 189–208, at 190–91.

32. Offe, "Challenging the Boundaries," 94.

33. Cunningham, *Democratic Theory*, 282–91.

34. *Ibid.*, 230–35. In brief, the reason to prescribe against this philosophical task is that it reinforces sectarianism by making judgments of political importance hinge on contested and, despite the confidence with which philosophers are wont to write, unproven and tentative high theory.

35. Though he does not make specific reference to applied ethics, one philosopher who articulates a position between moralism and foundational ethics, and who also puts his philosophical talents to the service of active radical politics, is Kai Nielsen. See the essays collected in his *Why Be Moral?* (Buffalo, NY: Prometheus Books, 1989).

36. Collins, *Rainbow Challenge*, 329.

37. Geras, "Ex-Marxism," 77, among other places.

38. Laclau and Mouffe, "Post-Marxism," 106.

39. I am abstracting from the complication that inter- and intramovement het-

erogeneity interpenetrate, since some people in one movement may share the antioppressive values of those in another, and movement memberships overlap; however, I believe that the comments below can be modified to accommodate this situation.

40. Carol Gould, *Rethinking Democracy: Freedom and Social Cooperation in Politics, Economy, and Society* (Cambridge: Cambridge University Press, 1988), chap. 3. Iris Marion Young, *Justice and the Politics of Difference*, chap. 6. Also pertinent is the effort of Laclau in *New Reflections*, see pts. 1, 3, and 4 therein, and Essay 7 of the present work.

41. A socialist philosopher as characterized in Essay 4 would therefore always be a "radical" philosopher; though radical philosophers are not by definition socialists. Political philosophers (or, indeed, speculative philosophers) who, in accord with the exhortations of Essay 5, strive to make their theories democracy enhancing specifically by means of combatting oppression would thereby infuse them with a radical dimension.

ESSAY 8

Democracy, Socialism, and the Globe

At a conference on "Democracy and Socialism" held in what was Yugo-slavia in 1989 and attended by about one hundred socialist theorists, most of the four days of animated discussion had to do with democracy, of which a bewildering number of definitions were offered.[1] At the end of the conference, someone observed that we had as yet to attempt defining "socialism." The suggestion was met with silence, and for good reason. The history of what called itself "real existing socialism" and its recent demise in Eastern Europe has now more than ever made this a contested concept. Assuming for the moment that the enormous task of rescuing the socialist ideal is worth undertaking, this requires concerted, innovative, historical, economic, and social-scientific work. Perhaps it also calls for philosophical inquiry into foundational ethics and social ontology. However, in keeping with the orientation of "middle-range" philosophy as described in the Preface, this essay applies conceptual analysis to real-life moral and politi-cal problems. Its arguments are advanced because there is at least

A version of this paper was published in Rodger Beehler, *et al.*, eds., *On the Track of Reason: Essays in Honor of Kai Nielsen* (Boulder, CO: Westview Press, 1992). Thanks are due to Hans Achterhuis and Roger Cotton for comments on an earlier draft. I have also profited from research and criticisms by Jean Carrière and David Slater, Centre for Latin American Research and Documentation (CEDLA), Amsterdam, and from discussions with fellow members of the Science for Peace Superordinate Project at the University of Toronto. Earlier versions of the paper were read in the Law Faculties at Hiroshima Shudo and Ritsumeikan Universities in Japan and in the Faculty of Philosophy at the University of Amsterdam.

one domain where the socialist ideal is most pressingly germane: the planet earth.

THE SOCIALIST IDEAL

By "the socialist ideal" I mean the core of those commonsense notions embodied in popular culture, recognized by both pro- and antisocialists, as well as by agnostics, to be that about socialism which its supporters think makes it worthy. Acknowledging debate over what this core idea is, or whether there is a single popular-cultural notion of socialism, a case has been made in earlier essays of this collection for equality as the core notion of the socialist ideal. It is with reference to equality that protagonists of socialism, ranging from social democrats to their revolutionary critics, have defended socialism, and that antisocialists have attacked it. Treatment of this subject in Essays 3 and 4 will not be repeated here, though some features of these treatments merit rehearsal.

First, a key strategy for making prescriptions about how to regard socialism is to distinguish among a socialist ideal, institutional means for realizing such an ideal, and movement-political organizations aiming to secure these institutions. Definitions of "socialism" by reference to state planning or social ownership of means of production (somehow interpreted) or workers' self-management pertain to alternative or complementary institutional arrangements. The notion of the dictatorship of the proletariat figures in a viewpoint about how to secure socialism and, if a Marxist distinction between socialism and communism is made, also in institutional considerations. Without denying the importance and difficulty of institutional and movement-political questions regarding global problems, this essay focuses, rather, on certain aspects of the socialist ideal. (It might be noted that at the 1989 conference in Yugoslavia, when people finally began to produce definitions, nobody proffered the dictatorship of the proletariat.)

Taken as an egalitarian ideal, to summarize a second feature, socialism is conceived of in terms of equality, modestly regarded. This means that rather than building into the ideal of socialism everything a socialist may value, it is thought of simply as the (presumptive) promotion of certain material equalities and regarded as one component of a project more important than itself—the democratic project—rather than as somehow embodying democracy in its essence. Real existing socialism's repeated declarations that it instantiated a concept of socialism as necessarily democratic did not inhibit and in fact supported its authoritarianism.

It might be asked whether, given the bad name socialism has acquired, the term should not simply be replaced by "egalitarianism." Briefly to summarize arguments given in other essays in this collection, the reason for resisting this is that the socialist ideal, as I conceive it, is not just proequality; it is also anticapitalist. Using arguments too well known to repeat here, the socialist maintains that capitalism gives some people disproportionate power to turn democratic decision-making procedures to their advantage, to violate them with impunity, and to prevent democratic progress. (Examples are, respectively, purchasing elections, bribery, and inhibiting electoral reform.)

Moreover, even given the political power that their economic freedom confers upon them, capitalists are themselves greatly constrained in the range of futures *they* can realistically strive to bring about due to pressures of competition. Perhaps small-scale capitalism is compatible with socialist values, but I consider it unfortunate that, due to its poor economic per-formance, formerly existing socialism seems to have turned so massively to capitalist principles of economic organization. Though it can only be stated as a still-untried hypothesis, I would still like to think that a dem-ocratic socialism would not be obliged to elicit economic innovation, dedi-cated management, and so on, by promising would-be entrepreneurs capitalist wealth.

"Democracy," as more thoroughly treated in Essay 3, applies to situations where people sharing some "environment"—a city, a nation, a family household, a geographic region, and so on—collectively strive to make it conform to their various preferences. Those modes of collective decision making, institutions, norms, and habits that facilitate success in this are to be preferred to alternatives from the point of view of democracy. Such modes will be context sensitive, as there is no one method that is always the best for protecting or advancing democracy. Furthermore, democracy is not something a society either entirely possesses or lacks, but is a matter of degree. The more people who have effective and ongoing control over a shared environment, the more democratic it is. Socialist equality is claimed to remove barriers to progress in democracy, of the sort, for instance, that prevent categories of people from effectively participating in democratic decision making.[2]

A third feature of socialism pertains to the understanding of material equality. In Essay 4, a "reactive" conception of equality was articulated, where the socialist egalitarian is most concerned to combat oppression. "Counteroppressive" socialist equality was there regarded as the provi-sion of material means to allow people the capacities and opportunities required to counteract the systematic and morally illegitimate thwarting of their aims. The approach followed in that essay was modest: to identify actual problems of grave inequality and to select principles appropriate to these problems. With respect to the globe, this task is, unfortunately, not difficult.

On a planet containing multimillionaires and affluent luxury for a relative few, subsistence living is the norm for the majority. Infant mortality, death from starvation, and disease directly related to malnutrition are the daily facts of life for people in much of Africa, Asia, and South America. While in the period between 1980 and 1985 the average annual income of those in the developed world was over $10,000 (U.S.), that of people in less-developed countries, in what is conventionally called the "third world," was less than $300.[3] Reflection on global inequality suggests that a broader conception than would be required for a universally adequate theory of equality should suffice. In particular, I think that the proposal by G. A. Cohen suffices. It will be recalled from the use made of Cohen's views in Essay 4 that for him what should be presumptively equalized are people's opportunities and capacities to enjoy what he calls "advantages," provided that deficiencies in opportunity or capacity are not of their own making.[4]

Perhaps there are some local circumstances or there will even come a time globally when it is important whether "advantage" is interpreted "hedonically," as that which actually does or would satisfy someone or in terms of preference satisfaction even when these are misguided; and as Cohen notes, it is sometimes difficult to identify which disadvantages are of one's own making, that is, result from one's uncoerced choices. But it is hard to imagine that people lack a preference to overcome chronic undernourishment, to secure educational and health-care facilities, and so on, or that they are somehow mistaken to have such preferences. Similarly, we have here clear cases where these disadvantages are not the results of the choices of those who endure them. This fact also suggests a virtue of Cohen's emphasis on opportunities and capacities. The main problem for a large portion of the world's population is not that they make bad life choices, but that their freedom to make effective choices about their future is severely constrained. Removal of these constraints would, accordingly, be a clear instance where equality and democracy are simultaneously furthered.

Global circumstances also dictate the *scope* of egalitarian considerations. Taking "scope" in one sense, the egalitarian must decide how much of any one person's life span is to be considered in determining his or her well-being. In another sense, the demographic boundaries toward which an egalitarian policy might be directed must be determined. Certain global considerations suggest that the appropriate scope for assessment of individual well-being should be long term and that the appropriate population should include future generations of humans (and perhaps present and future generations of nonhuman species as well). The global features to which I refer are, of course, those that make up the current ecological crisis. "Greenhouse" or global-warming effects are starting to be felt. The ozone layer is already punctured. Rainforests are being destroyed at a rate of fifteen million hectares per year (which on one estimate will make them extinct by 2040).[5] Nuclear waste accumulates without any realistic proposals about its safe disposal. People are being choked and poisoned to death by pollution in every large city in the world. In the remainder of this paper, I shall further articulate a democratic-socialist position by relating it to the ecological crisis and to global inequality with reference to an important recent initiative.

GLOBAL MACROPROBLEMS AND THE BRUNTLAND REPORT

Thanks to their stark reality, it is now recognized as incumbent on any approach to global politics (a) to combat global inequality; (b) to create an ecologically secure world; and (c) to address (a) and (b) at the same time. Earlier thinking about these matters either took the overly optimistic perspective, sometimes associated with the notion of a "technological fix," according to which (b) was a pseudo-problem, since technology could correct both social and technological problems. Or, the "limits to growth" perspective associated with the Club of Rome took a pessimistic view, especially regarding problem (c). Only a world freeze on industrial development could sustain future life on the planet, even though this freeze would be especially disadvantageous to the underdeveloped world.[6] The more recent and more thoughtful initiative is that of the United Nations World Commission on Environment and Development, expressed in its report, *Our Common Future*, often called by the name of the Commission's chair, Gro Harlem Bruntland.[7]

The Bruntland Report correctly identifies world poverty as one of the principal causes of the ecological crisis. Poverty drives people to engage or acquiesce in ecologically destructive activities, for instance, those leading to deforestation. Poverty also creates political instability which obstructs cooperative worldwide action and, being war prone, fuels the diversion of much-needed resources into military expenditures, not to mention the destruction caused by wars themselves. In a now-celebrated phrase, the report calls for concerted and coordinated effort for "sustainable development," whereby humanity will "ensure that it meets the needs of the present without compromising the ability of future generations to meet their own needs."[8] The concept of sustainable development is sufficiently vague to admit of several interpretations, and sometimes its goals are at least in the direction of what a socialist could accept.[9]

In its "realistic" moments, however, the Bruntland Report largely relies on the private sector: "In practice, and in the absence of global management of the economy or the environment, attention must be focussed on the improvement of policies in areas where the scope for cooperation is already defined: aid, trade, transnational corporations, and technological transfer."[10] Little is said about how this is to be done, except to note regarding aid that "the World Bank can support environmentally sound projects and policies. In financing structural adjustment, the International Monetary Fund should support wider and longer term development objectives than at present."[11] And, despite acknowledgment of the lack of trust of developing countries toward the transnationals due to "an asymmetry in bargaining power," the report urges less-developed host countries and transnational corporations to "share responsibilities" to preserve resources and the environment.[12]

One way to read the Bruntland Report (and in terms of inferring the actual motivation of its authors, I am inclined to think this a probable reading) is as a plea for those whom it correctly sees as holding overwhelming power in matters of the world economy—transnational corporations and procapitalist monetary agencies—to pursue more ecological and egalitarian policies (partly by assuring them that this is consistent with the continued pursuit of profit),[13] while also urging international bodies to take a more active role in controlling these forces. However, due in part to its vagueness, the report admits of an alternative combining elements of global welfarism and free-market, supply-side economic policy.

A welfarist reading is consistent with the Bruntland Report's implied definition of equality by reference to "needs." On one view, needs are social constructs, and so appeal to them is an illusory form of objectivity.[14] In addition, depending on what is admitted as a need, satisfaction of needs is not enough to empower people to take full control of their lives. In the report it is allowed that there are needs for "education" and "health" and that beyond basic needs is one for an "improved quality of life." But in its most focused treatment, the report calls for satisfaction of "the essential needs of the world's poor," examples of which are food, clothing, shelter, and jobs.[15] Due to the abysmal state of the world's poor, it would be no small gain if these things were secured, but given that people require little simply to survive, and that a hard and demeaning job is still a job, it would be deceptive to describe policies that went no further than this as sufficient.

A free-market reading is compatible with the Bruntland Report's several references to the central role of the World Bank and the International Monetary Fund. Increasingly, these institutions have integrated aid with "structural adjustment packages" by which aid is conditional on such things as lowering trade barriers, reducing government expenditures on social services, restricting money supply, raising interest rates, and other measures designed to improve trade balances within a strengthened free-enterprise environment.[16] One justification for this has been that an international free market is supposed eventually to raise third world living standards. This is a highly dubious claim. Relatively unhindered third world investment opportunities for transnational corporations have existed throughout this century, but the gap between it and the first world has not shrunk. While the difference between average incomes in rich countries exceeded that in poor ones by a ratio of 20 to 1 in 1960, by 1980 it had increased to 46 to 1.[17] In the period 1980–1987, average per capita incomes fell by 16 percent in Latin America and the Caribbean and by 30 percent in sub-Saharan Africa.[18]

It seems clear that the possibility of such procapitalist readings of the Bruntland Report's recommendations explains its support by some of the world's largest capitalist concerns. For instance, the U.N.'s conference, Globe 90, held in Vancouver to promote the report, included representatives from Dow Chemical, Mitsubishi, Esso, British Nuclear Fuels, Hitachi, Weyerhauser, and several others of the same sort.[19] Even if one imputed noble intentions to such economic agents, and even if they put aside their free-market policies, I do not think that a project under capitalist hegemony could successfully confront the global problems. This would require more coordination and profit-risking sacrifice than can be expected from capitalist enterprises. It is for this reason that a noncapitalist alternative is urgently required.

A SOCIALIST ALTERNATIVE

Since publication of the Bruntland Report, there have been many critiques by experts on development and by ecologists, each either modifying or offering an alternative to Bruntland's definition of "sustainable development."[20]

Many ecologists restrict themselves to the term "sustainability" in order to avoid the technocratic, growth-ethic connotations of "development." Though sympathetic with this motive, I favour retaining the original phrase because this now widely used term is associated more with the Bruntland Commission's astute identification of ecological and economic macroproblems than with any one interpretation of this phrase. This makes it an important focus for the sort of hegemonic political struggle appropriately advocated by many democratic socialist theorists. (In terms of this neo-Gramscian approach, sustainable development is a floating signifier, susceptible to articulation either around egalitarian or capitalist projects.)[21]

Borrowing from Bruntland and in light of the earlier discussion about equality, "sustainable development" should be thought of as a worldwide effort to promote equality of those opportunities and capacities required for people in both present and future generations to pursue a meaningful life as they see it. The term "meaningful life" is central to the proposal for a proactive conception of socialist equality to supplement the reactive, counteroppressive notion referred to above, while recognizing that in actual socialist politics and policy implementation the two will interact. Its intent is to capture the idea that one is looking to ensure more than short-term satisfaction or equality of unsatisfactory lives. Cohen's rider to his "equality" definition about removing impediments that have not resulted from one's choice is supposed in this conception, but with a focus on the pressing need to rectify inequalities of opportunity and capacity that have been imposed on the world's poor or that we are in the process of imposing on following generations.

Use of the philosophically loaded term "meaningful" aims to capture something of Macpherson's focus, summarized in Essay 1, on development of people's potentials to lead intrinsically worthwhile lives as an alternative to a possessive individualist ethos of unbridled consumption. At the same time, and reflecting worries expressed in that essay, the subjective rider, "as they see it," is included to ensure that appeal to sustainable development not be paternalistically employed. This means that neither existing conventions of one's society nor some philosophical theory of ethics or human nature can decisively preclude success in pursuit of an idiosyncratic lifestyle from counting as meaningful, but I do not think this makes meaningfulness entirely arbitrary or capricious either.

In brief (and counting on continuing progress by egalitarians more skilled than I in addressing the philosophical fine points around this question),[22] claims about what makes one's life meaningful are not like announcements of simple and short-term preferences; more is needed to justify a polity's allocation of resources to its promotion. Such a polity would not, it seems to me, be acting in an objectionable paternalistic way if it denied allocation to someone whose life plan was incoherent, hopelessly unrealistic, or blatantly harmful to others. Of course, there are both philosophical problems and political dangers involved in deciding what is coherent, realistic, or harmful, but I suspect that these problems seem more insurmountable in the abstract than when confronted on a case-by-case basis in specific social circumstances.

As in the case of the discussion of counteroppressive equality in Essay 4, one reason to make democratic progress is that democratic institutions and cultures encourage the tolerance required to counteract attempts at stifling unconventional life-styles, and they provide fertile ground within which candidates for a good life can be experimented with, discussed, debated, and, in general, examined. Promoting democracy, seeking the good, and equalizing life's benefits and burdens on this perspective are thus regarded as mutually affecting activities that have the potential to combine in upward spirals. It is when democracy, the good, and equality are viewed abstractly (that is, statically and out of specific contexts) that relating them seems an insurmountable problem.[23]

In addition to prescribing this socialist-ideal conception of sustainable development, it is also here urged that activities to promote sustainability be carried on in a socialistic way. By this I mean, on the one hand, that capitalist-serving interpretations of sustainable development and limitations of the range of solutions to global problems be vigorously resisted and, on the other hand, that champions of sustainable development have no illusions about its compatibility with capitalism. Instead, one should proceed on the presumption that effective measures for sustainability must be *forced* on capitalists and on procapitalist governments. Among other measures, this means exerting political pressure on one's own and, where feasible, on other governments to pass and enforce effective laws; encouraging the integration of sustainable developmental attitudes and demands within social movements (such as labour unions) that have some power with respect to capitalist enterprises; extending active political, economic, and moral support to national liberation movements; mobilizing local and international support (in one's professional or work circles, for instance) to strengthen international agencies like the U.N. and international law;[24] and engaging in more direct measures like mass demonstrations or boycotts.

NATIONAL SOVEREIGNTY AND POPULAR VALUES

I wish to return to the question of how realistic a socialist approach to sustainable development is. But first I must disclaim adherence to a view found among some socialists that capitalism is not only *an* obstacle to worthy pursuits, but that it is the *only* serious obstacle. Any effort to make significant progress in sustainable development requires overcoming difficulties that would exist even if capitalist obstacles were neutralized. Two of these merit special mention: the problem of national sovereignty and the problem of popular values.

The first problem is that nation states are the loci of most macro–decision making, which renders international cooperation difficult and creates a situation where each nation fears its sovereignty will be threatened if it unilaterally takes measures toward sustainability. The second problem is that, unless one implausibly and dangerously postulates a benevolent ecodictator,[25] sustainable development will necessitate at least passive popular support. This means a transformation of values, especially of those in the developed world, who must reject consumerist values.[26] Let me now suggest that solutions to these problems are to be found in considerations of democracy.

Regarding each problem, it is worth noting that we do not face an entirely hopeless situation. To be sure, national sovereignty is fiercely defended, but at the same time there are examples of transfer of national power to transnational authority, perhaps most dramatically in the case of the emerging European Community. Similarly, not everyone in the developed world eagerly embraces consumerist values or is callous toward the plight of the deprived. In particular, many social movements—ecological, peace, women's, and others—have actively promoted alternatives to consumerism and a more caring stance toward the developing world. In the fall of 1990, for instance, the Canadian Auto Workers Union negotiated a contract that obliged management to contribute to a union fund for third world relief.

My point is not that the European Community is necessarily a force for sustainable development or that the social movements represent majority opinion, but that they offer evidence for voluntary relinquishing of sovereignty and for cultural transformation. What is actual must be possible. We might also remind ourselves that the first world is no longer able to isolate itself from its ecological and economic effects on the third. The Persian Gulf War was largely a Frankenstein's Monster. Exploitation of third world workers creates unemployment in the first world and the social and economic strains of forced migration. Destructive ecological practices are felt worldwide.

Democratic solutions to the problems of national sovereignty and popular consciousness appeal to the broad concept of democracy alluded to above. Not being confined just to representative government and formal decision making at the level of states, democratic politics also encourages local, participatory democracy. As nearly all ecologists urge, this is essential for replacing antiecological mass society and associated values with more self-sufficient societies whose members value community over consumerism.[27] At the same time, since democracy applies to any social environment in which the behaviour of some people affects others in an ongoing way, it is appropriate to extend formal and informal democratic decision making and democratic values (like mutual toleration and respect for democratic rights) beyond national boundaries to regions and to the entire globe.

Democratic politics, then, is a matter of overcoming obstacles to collective self-determination—including those posed by capitalism and by selfish and short-sighted nationalism—at all levels where people interact. That such politics has the potential to promote sustainable development is a hypothesis that needs to be put to the test. I shall sharpen the hypothesis by suggesting frameworks for solutions to each of the two problems under discussion.

Global Equal Partnership

Regarding national sovereignty, the hypothesis suggests one way that democratic politics is essential to sustainable development. That the third world and the developed world confront a nest of common macroproblems is undeniable. Hence, they form a single entity, between the two main parts of which, as the Bruntland Report rightly urges, coordinated actions are urgently required. Assuming that such actions are more effective when they have popular support than when they are imposed, then democratic involvement of the people in question is required. However, these people are divided into two categories, neither possessing sufficient democratic control over globe-related policy and between whom there is a giant imbalance of wealth. Thus, a politics to increase popular input to such policy in the developed world must be conjoined with a demand that the policy include *unilateral* action for support of the third world. The reason for this is plain.

Partnership in the confrontation of shared problems requires mutual trust between the partners. Evidently, such trust is justifiably lacking on the part of third world peoples, and only dramatic initiatives in the developed world can earn it. In addition, antidemocratic structures in the third world often impede popular involvement in policy matters. If effective confrontation of macroproblems requires general democratic support, then it is in the interests of people in the developed world to facilitate democratic progress in the third. Since main impediments to such progress derive, sometimes quite directly,[28] from the activities of developed-world economic and political forces, democratic politics in the developed world to curtail these forces can significantly contribute to third world democracy.

Possessive Individualism and a Global Community

Democratic theorists have done useful work to explain how efforts to gain control over some aspect of one's life lead people to democratic struggle, which in turn creates in them prodemocratic attitudes.[29] While it seems to me that this general pattern of explanation also applies to the possibility of "cultural revolutions" in the interests of sustainable development, additional considerations are required with reference to global problems. On the one hand, the culture of selfishness and consumerism, what Macpherson called "possessive individualism," must be overcome. This is at least a necessary condition for promoting global and transgenerational equality. On the other hand, people must actually value such equality.

I confess to insecurity about how to conceptualize ways that the needed cultural revolutions might be facilitated. My intuition is that the answer requires examination of those places where questions of democracy intersect with questions about the meaning of life. Macpherson hypothesized that the original democratic impulse was for human empowerment, where this meant that individuals would possess the means to develop their "truly human potentials" (for such things as creativity or friendship). Under conditions of life in a competitive market society, however, this ambition was thwarted, and a possessive individualist culture according with such a society came to dominate.

Despite its pervasiveness, Macpherson thought that possessive individualism never completely replaced the original democratic impulse and that it is *because* people are blocked from developing their potentials that, by default, they act in accord with selfish and consumerist values. A meaningful life would be one where people actively develop their talents rather than passively accumulate goods.[30] If Macpherson was right,[31] then it is insufficient democratic empowerment that sustains a possessive-individualist culture, and democracy-enhancing politics should therefore work against this culture.

Somewhat different considerations apply in the case of valuing global and transgenerational equality. Recent work by communitarians such as Michael Walzer, Alasdair MacIntyre, and the others discussed in Essay 6 offers a clue. Communitarians criticize modern liberalism for reflecting and promoting a hyperindividualistic view of people, whereby they are cut off from the religious, national, ethnic, and other community traditions that define their identities and give their lives a sense of purpose. Individualist critics have challenged the communitarians with antidemocracy, citing the importance for democracy—recognized at least since the major democratic revolutions of the eighteenth and nineteenth centuries—of challenging tradition. Those communitarians discussed in Essay 6 have responded by urging that there is room within traditions to sanction their own critique.[32] On this view, democracy and tradition are compatible if demands of the former can alter traditions without obliterating them. More germane to present purposes is the possibility that, confronted with democratic pressures, the way that traditions change is to enlarge their scope.

One feature of communities is that people who gain a sense of identity from them seek goals geographically and temporally beyond their own persons. It is important to community members that their religious community, nation, or family survive beyond them; and they feel they have done something valuable and personally rewarding if they have contributed to this end, even to the point of making sacrifices. To be sure, this propensity, when combined with intolerance, yields fanaticism and is often manipulated to evil purpose. However, when confronted with the democratic demand for mutual tolerance and the promotion of cross-community democracy (in particular, of the sort suggested above in respect to partnership between the developed and the third world), one possible effect is for community members to extend the boundaries of what they consider a community worth preserving.[33]

If the boundaries of very many communities were fixed and internally homogeneous, this would be unrealistic, but few communities match this description. Also, there are actual instances of such extensions, for example reflected in the solidarity many churches have expressed with those engaged in national liberation struggles, or when there is international aid in response to disasters. To the extent that this possibility exists, a democratic politics that simultaneously defends community traditions, combats intolerant attitudes within a community, and supports intercommunity mutual understanding and cooperation should contribute to a transformation of values supportive of sustainable development.

SOCIALIST REVOLUTION

This essay began by arguing for the rescue of the socialist ideal, interpreted in an egalitarian manner. To an imagined query, "why not simply advocate egalitarianism?," it was responded, it is important to retain the notion of socialism because of its explicitly anticapitalist connotations. This invites the objection, implied in the Bruntland Report's justification of its reliance on transnational corporations, that the prescribed approach is unrealistic. It might be claimed that, according to this democratic-socialist orientation, sustainable development requires worldwide socialism, but even if this were ever feasible, global macroproblems are too pressing to await it.

This objection would have force against an approach to socialism whereby socialist state victory is seen as a necessary forerunner for making any democratic progress. But socialism as I regard it is just the egalitarian moment within democratic politics. Any policy, practice, or economic or political institutions that promote equality along the lines indicated above may be regarded as socialistic. In the course of efforts to make progress in democracy, inegalitarian impediments are so often encountered that socialist politics are always appropriate. If there is a "chicken and egg" problem, it is not that socialist equality is required for sustainable development, but that democracy is required for democracy. That is, democratic politics is required to overcome antidemocratic impediments to sustainability. Rather than seeing this as an argument for the impossibility of democratic politics, I view what successes there have been in democratic politics as evidence that democracy is a potentially self-building process.

Perhaps the worst effects of the global crises we have been addressing can be staved off in part by containing and counteracting the most powerful capitalist interests. However, for those sceptical of this potential and in light of the high stakes involved, such politics are not enough and the world will not be secure until the economies of at least significant portions of it have been restructured in an egalitarian way, compatibly with a democratic transformation of global values: thus the urgency of democratic-socialist politics and the socialist ideal.

Notes

1. The conference was held in Cavtat, Yugoslavia, October 19–22, 1989, under the auspices of the journal *Socialism in the World*. While there was an undertaking to publish taped discussions in the journal, subsequent events in that country have apparently intervened to cancel this project.
2. The fullest treatment of democracy, as discussed in Essay 3, may be found in my *Democratic Theory and Socialism* (Cambridge: Cambridge University Press, 1987), chap. 3, along with references to alternative and complementary theories.
3. F. E. Trainer, "Reconstructing Radical Develoment Theory," *Alternatives*, Vol. 14, No. 4 (October 1989), 481–515, see 487, and his many references.
4. G. A. Cohen's, "On the Currency of Egalitarian Justice," *Ethics*, Vol. 99, No. 4 (July 1989), 906–44.
5. These figures are calculated by Trainer, "Development Theory," 502. He uses data of N. Guppy, "Tropical Deforestation: A Global View," *Foreign Affairs*, Vol. 4 (Spring 1984), 928–66.
6. The Club of Rome position was summarized in D. Meadows, *et al.*, *The Limits to Growth* (New York: Universe Books, 1972). I believe the term "technological fix" was coined by Alvin Weinberg, "Can Technology Replace Social Engineering?" *University of Chicago Magazine*, No. 59 (October 1966), 6–10.
7. World Commission on Environment and Development, *Our Common Future* (Oxford: Oxford University Press, 1987), and in several other languages.
8. *Our Common Future*, 8.
9. For example, "developing countries must operate in a world in which the resources gap between most developing and industrial nations is widening, in which the industrial world dominates in the rule making of some key international bodies, and in which the industrial world has already used up much of the planet's ecological capital. This inequality is the planet's main 'environmental' problem; it is also its main 'development' problem" (*ibid.*, 5–6). Socialist modifications to this passage would begin by identifying as among the major figures in the "industrial world" its large capitalist firms, and by arguing that specifically anticapitalist measures are required.
10. *Our Common Future*, 75–76.
11. *Ibid.*, 18.
12. *Ibid.*, 86.
13. For example: "For their part, many corporations have recognized the need to share managerial skills and technological know-how with host-country nationals and to pursue profit-seeking objectives within a framework of long-term sustainable development," *Our Common Future*, 85–86. Or consider the assertion in one of the short-form summaries of the report that "[transnational corporations] can have a significant impact on the environment and resources of other countries and should pursue their profit objectives within a framework of long-term sustainable development," *Sustainable Development: A Guide to Our Common Future*, prepared by G. Lebel and H. Kane (Oxford: Oxford University Press, 1987), 8.
14. Pertinent critiques of the concept of "need" are J. Baudrillard, *For a Critique of the*

Political Economy of the Sign (St. Louis, MO: Telos, 1981), 63–87, and C. B. Macpherson, "Needs and Wants: An Ontological or Historical Problem," in Ross Fitzgerald, ed., *Human Needs and Politics* (New York: Pergamon Press, 1977), 26–35. It may be possible to construct a theory of needs that retains both their objectivity and relativity. An effort in this direction is by David Braybrooke, *Meeting Needs* (Princeton, NJ: Princeton University Press, 1987). Similar considerations attach to the notion of "scarcity," which, like "need," is often used as if it were a historically unconstructed concept. A critique of the notion of "scarcity" analogous to those of needs is by Hans Achterhuis, *Het rijk van de schaarste* (Utrecht: Ambo, 1988).

15. *Our Common Future*, 43ff.

16. See Dharam Ghai and Cynthia Hewitt de Alcantara, "The Crisis of the 1980s in Sub-Saharan Africa, Latin America and the Caribbean: Economic Impact, Social Change and Political Implications," *Development and Change*, Vol. 21, No. 3 (July 1990), 389–426, at 403, and Cheryl Payer, *The World Bank: A Critical Analysis* (New York: Monthly Review Press, 1982).

17. T. McGowan and B. Kordan, "Imperialism in World System Perspective," *International Studies Quarterly*, Vol. 25, No. 1 (March 1981), 43–68, cited in Trainer "Development Theory," 487.

18. Ghai and de Alcantara, "Crisis of the 1980s", 391–401. They use World Bank statistics. See, too, the sustained attack on market solutions to developing-world problems by Trainer, "Development Theory," Also relevant is Michael Redclift's *Sustainable Development: Exploring the Contradictions* (London: Methuen, 1987), chap. 5. Advocates of free-market, "trickle-down theory," like the American former Reagan advisor Francis Fukuyama (*The Guardian* [September 7, 1990], 3), like to point to the "Four Tigers" (Hong Kong, Taiwan, Singapore, and South Korea) as evidence for their position, but they fail to note that these "Tigers" total only 2 percent of the third world's population, that there are already strains on their limited-product, export-oriented economies, and that what "success" they have enjoyed has been accompanied by appalling conditions of work and enormous debts. See Trainer, 487–88, and Redclift, 100–101, and their references.

19. Reported in the editorial by Larry Lohmann in *The Ecologist*, Vol. 20, No. 3 (May/June 1990), 82–84.

20. Alternative definitions are discussed by W. M. Adams, *Green Development: Environment and Sustainability in the Third World* (London: Routledge, 1990), chaps. 3 and 9.

21. See Ernesto Laclau and Chantal Mouffe, *Hegemony and Socialist Strategy* (London: Verso, 1985), 105–33, for an explication of the theory behind this sort of approach. Pertinent works are by Robert Cox, *Production, Power and World Order* (New York: Columbia University Press, 1987), and Enrico Augelli ans Craig Murphy, *America's Quest for Supremacy and the Third World: A Gramscian Analysis* (London: Pinter Publishers, 1988).

22. The central problem is the one discussed in Essay 4 about finding a way coherently to combine both objective and subjective considerations in making prescriptions about what should be equalized. G. A. Cohen is one egalitarian theorist who fruitfully approaches this topic, and in the article referred to in note 4 he cites several additional authors (Richard Arneson, Ronald Dworkin, T. M. Scanlon, Amartya Sen, and others) who, from different perspectives and with

different emphases, seem to me nonetheless collectively to be asymptotically approaching a solution to this and related problems.

23. Macpherson articulates and defends such an interactive viewpoint in *The Life and Times of Liberal Democracy* (Oxford: Oxford University Press, 1977), 98–108.

24. One environmental lawyer suggests, for example, that the weak Article XX(6) of the General Agreement on Tariffs and Trade (GATT) be amended to allow countries to exempt national policies designed to protect their environment from restrictions on national policy provided for under the Agreement. See Steven Shrybman, "International Trade and the Environment," *Alternatives*, Vol. 17, No. 2 (July/August 1990), 20–29. In general, international environmental law and agencies to enforce it need to be greatly strengthened. Appropriate suggestions are by Douglas M. Johnston, "Systemic Environmental Damage: The Challenge to International Law and Organization," *Syracuse Journal of International Law and Commerce*, No. 225 (1985), 45–71, and Sharon Williams, "Public International Law Governing Transboundary Pollution," *University of Queensland Law Journal*, No. 112 (1984), 17–41.

25. The attitude that ecodictatorship may be, if not desirable, perhaps inevitable, strikes me as pernicious in the extreme. It is exactly analogous to arguments that were given to defend Stalinism, and would likely have the same effect: They would work against the goals they are supposed to promote. The reason for this is that there are powerful vested interests that stand to lose if effective egalitarian and ecological measures are instituted on a worldwide scale. A would-be ecodictator would therefore have to marshal sufficient counterforces against anticipated resistance. The only apparent counterforce is in the power of numbers of the world's majority populations. But it is hard to see how a dictator could gain or sustain such support. Indeed, far more likely is that ecodictators would either be overwhelmed or co-opted by minority interests. Although he does not endorse ecodictatorship, Redclift expresses the frustration of many environmentalists: "[T]he argument could be put that containing economic demands for material advance, in a highly unequal world, requires political measures that are so authoritarian they would immediately contradict the liberating, humane objectives that would make development sustainable in the first place," *Sustainable Development*, 199–200.

26. Patricia Mische puts the point well: "A total systems approach to global ecological security involves many interacting forces [including]: 1) a strong and effective global polity including strengthened international environmental law, adjudication, and compliance; and 2) a global culture of ecological responsibility. While the former is important, I consider the latter utterly indispensable. It is also essential to the effectiveness of the first," "Ecological Security and the Need to Reconceptualize Sovereignty," *Alternatives*, Vol. 14, No. 4 (October 1989), 389–427, at 413.

27. Thus Trainer lists as the imperatives for the developing world: "Decentralize. Democratize. Devolve control to local regions and villages," "Development Theory," 506.

28. Noam Chomsky's heavily documented accounts are apt: *Turning the Tide: The U.S. and Latin America* (Montreal: Black Rose Books, 1986), and *The Washington Connection and Third World Fascism*, coauthored with Edward Herman (Montreal: Black Rose Books, 1979).

29. Laclau and Mouffe (*Hegemony*, chap. 4) distinguish two sources of transformation of values in a prodemocratic way: those created in struggle to realize democratic rights, and those created in efforts to overcome oppression.
30. Essay 1 of this collection discusses Macpherson's views relevant to this topic. Key texts pertinent to the point are: *Democratic Theory: Essays in Retrieval* (Oxford: Oxford University Press, 1973), and *The Life and Times of Liberal Democracy*.
31. Annually for the last eighteen years, I have taught a course in philosophy to about 300 first-year engineering students, to whom I put the following question (modelled on Aristotle's alternative interpretations of "happiness"): Suppose that you had a (mutually exclusive) choice between (a) finding an affordable way to harness the sun's energy on a large scale, or one or more of (b) fame; (c) fortune; and (d) power. The large majority have always selected (a). Since in North America these are famously outspoken students who like to shock their left-wing and liberal professors, I conclude that they mean this, and that the reason most will actually pursue (b) through (d) instead is that very few of them are ever afforded an opportunity to exercise their talents in such causes.
32. Two texts that explicitly address the relation between community values and democratic tolerance are: Alasdair MacIntyre, *Whose Justice? Which Rationality?* (Notre Dame, IN: University of Notre Dame Press, 1988), see 361–62, 387–88, and Michael Walzer, *The Company of Critics: Social Criticism and Political Commitment in the 20th Century* (New York: Basic Books, 1988).
33. This includes temporal and not just spatial extensions. Studies of the ethics of obligations to future generations which bear on this argument are: Daniel Callahan, "What Obligations Do We Have to Future Generations?" and Gregory Kavka, "The Futurity Problem," in Ernest Partridge, ed., *Responsibilities to Future Generations* (Buffalo, NY: Prometheus Books, 1987).

Index